CODENAMED DORSET

GVI RI

This scroll commemorates

Major C. M. Ogden-Smith
Royal Regiment of Artillery

held in honour as one who
served King and Country in
the world war of 1939-1945
and gave his life to save
mankind from tyranny. May
his sacrifice help to bring
the peace and freedom for
which he died.

CODENAMED DORSET

The Wartime Exploits of
Major Colin Ogden-Smith

Commando & SOE

Peter Jacobs

FRONTLINE BOOKS, LONDON

FRONTLINE BOOKS, LONDON

Codenamed Dorset: The Wartime Exploits of Major Colin Ogden-Smith

This edition published in 2014 by Frontline Books, an imprint of
Pen & Sword Books Limited, 47 Church Street, Barnsley, S. Yorkshire, S70 2AS
www.frontline-books.com

ISBN: 978-1-84832-686-6

CIP data records for this title are available from the British Library
and the Library of Congress

For more information on our books, please visit
www.frontline-books.com,
email info@frontline-books.com
or write to us at the above address.

Typeset by JCS Publishing Services Ltd, www.jcs-publishing.co.uk in Caslon Pro font
(12.5pt on 15pt)

Printed in Great Britain by CPI Group (UK) Ltd, Croydon, CR0 4YY

*To Charmian, Colin's daughter, who would have loved
to read this book but sadly will not get the chance*

Also, in memory of Colin's friends, none of whom lived to see the freedom they had all fought so gallantly for:

Lieutenant Donald Percy Passmore – Died of Wounds 21 April 1941

Captain Frank Raymond Jocelyn Nicholls – Killed in Action 11 May 1942

Major Gustavus Henry March-Phillipps DSO MBE – Killed in Action 12 September 1942

Major John Geoffrey Appleyard DSO MC* – Killed in Action 13 July 1943

Captain Graham Hayes MC – Executed 13 July 1943

Captain Philip Hugh Pinckney – Killed in Action 7 September 1943

Captain Patrick Laurence Dudgeon MC – Killed in Action 3 October 1943

Captain Derek John Plantagenet Thirkell-White – Killed in Action 14/15 November 1943

Captain Thomas Anthony Mellows – Died of Wounds 21 August 1944

Captain Jocelyn Fulke Dalrymple Radice – Died of Wounds 27 August 1944

Captain Victor Albert Gough – Executed 25 November 1944

Major Anders Frederick Emil V Schau Lassen VC MC** – Killed in Action 9 April 1945

Contents

Illustrations

Plates

A Message from the Mayor Of Querrien, Brittany, France

1.   Marcel Moysan, Mayor of Querrien 1995–2014.

As the Mayor of Querrien, I want to certify the closeness of our local community to the memory of Major Colin Ogden-Smith, who died bravely seventy years ago with two other men.

Those who met him during July 1944 speak of his particular affection for the Breton people as the family who welcomed him into their homes and wished for him to return again after the war. Sadly, his destiny was to die and to rest in peace forever in the land of Brittany that he had helped to liberate. With a French SAS man, he faced the enemy and sacrificed his life to allow the rest of his team to escape.

As the leader of the Jedburgh team his courage and bravery have made him a great hero to us all and we have admired what he did for the past seventy years. Every two years we commemorate together beside the two crosses erected in memory of the three men who died heroically there. The younger generations must also remember them to appreciate that they can live peacefully now after the sacrifices made by so many people.

I am sure this book will also contribute towards keeping alive the memory of our fallen hero, Colin Ogden-Smith, and I am grateful to the author, Peter Jacobs, for his fantastic engagement and passion to preserve the legacy and tragedy of Kerbozec.

Marcel Moysan
Mayor of Querrien

Acknowledgements

I T WOULD NOT HAVE been possible to tell a story such as this without the help of so many people over several years. It is difficult to know where to start but, as I have to start somewhere, I will start with where the story first began for me.

My interest in Colin Ogden-Smith started in 2006 following an auction of military medals held in London. Although I was unable to get to London on the day, Colin's medals came to me via my good friend Richard Black, one of the leading dealers of British gallantry and campaign medals in the world. With the medals came a large quantity of original photographs and very poignant letters that had been sent to the Ogden-Smith family from people in France after Colin had been killed, and it was while reading these letters that I was immediately drawn to the emotiveness of this story.

For the next four years I simply researched as much as I could. At that stage it was purely for personal reasons so that I could understand a bit more about the man behind the medals. My research took me to the Whitgift School in Croydon, where Colin and his two brothers, Tony and Bruce, were educated. My initial correspondence was through the Old Whitgiftians Association and so I must thank Nigel Platts for getting me started. Nigel then put me in touch with the school's archivist, William Wood, who has always willingly helped me in any way he can and also made me so very welcome during my visit to the school. My research also took me to the Honourable Artillery Company. All three Ogden-Smith brothers were members of the HAC in the years leading up to the

2. The medals awarded to Major Colin Ogden-Smith and the inspiration behind *Codenamed Dorset*. The medals are (from left-right): 1939-45 Star; Africa Star; France and Germany Star; Defence Medal; War Medal 1939-45 (with oak leaf for Mention in Despatches); Territorial Efficiency Decoration.

Second World War and so I must thank Justine Taylor, the archivist of the HAC, for all her help. I have also been pleased to communicate with others from the HAC, including Paul Champness and Simon Waters. It is only limited space that prevents me from writing more about Colin's earlier life – both during his time at the Whitgift and as a member of the HAC – but many thanks, once again, to those at the school and at the HAC.

Another to have helped me was William Craven at the Estates Office at Milton Hall. The Fitzwilliam family kindly allowed me to visit Milton Hall and I am particularly grateful to William for taking the time to show me around parts of the estate where the Jedburgh Training School was set up in 1944. I am also grateful to a colleague of mine, Trevor Hopper, for passing on his knowledge of morphine so that I could better understand how it was used by special forces during the Second World War. While this might seem an unusual thing to mention before reading the book, this proved extremely helpful for me when trying to understand the final few moments of Colin's life.

But what really enabled me to take my research to another level came after I posted a message on John Robertson's Special Forces website, appealing for any information relating to Colin. The response was incredible. First of all I had some most interesting e-mails from Ned Malet in Jersey, Mike Booker in France and also from Cherry Cane. All three were able to provide me with useful information about Colin and so I would like to take this opportunity to thank them all. I must also thank John Robertson on behalf of all enthusiasts and historians for running his excellent website, without which stories such as this could never be told.

The more I learned about the courage of Colin Ogden-Smith, and about the depth of gratitude that still lives on in the local community in Brittany where he gave his life for the liberation of France, the more I felt the story needed to be told. The first of two major breakthroughs came when Sam Gardner, the granddaughter of Bruce Ogden-Smith, made contact with me using the information on John's Special Forces website. This took me directly to the Ogden-Smith family and specifically to Sam's mother, Angela Weston, who, in turn, helped me take my research to yet another level. Having met with Angela, she kindly put me in contact with Colin's daughter, Charmian Musgrove. Charmian was delighted to learn that a book was being written about her father and during the following year we met on a number of occasions at her home near Arundel in West Sussex, and spent many hours on the telephone. She had been just seven months old when her father had been killed and so she was understandably fascinated to learn so much about him. She also had some photographs and letters, as well as some research that had been put together after the war, and between us we were able to slowly piece together her father's wartime exploits.

In the meantime, Angela had also put me in contact with her other cousin, Annie Bland, the daughter of Colin's older brother, Tony, and so I was also delighted to meet with Annie. In the space of just a few months I had met all three daughters of the three Ogden-Smith brothers. I found that quite remarkable and it had all been made possible through Sam Gardner's initial e-mail, which, in turn, was due to John Robertson's Special Forces website. Thanks, Sam, for taking the time to make that first contact and for all your help providing me with much-needed translations between French and English. Sadly, though, Charmian will not get the chance to read this book. She died suddenly in 2012, but I take comfort in knowing that she would have been pleased with the end product.

Through that same Special Forces forum I had also made contact with the family of Arthur Dallow, Colin's radio operator in France. This was initially through his two grandsons, Tom Taig in Australia and Matt Dallow here in England, and through them both I was able to make contact with Arthur's two daughters, Ann and Elizabeth. Both have provided me with useful information about their father and I was delighted to be able to meet up and enjoy lunch with Elizabeth and Matt, and so many thanks to all those of the Dallow family who have provided me with their help.

I had all the information I needed from this side of the Channel but I could never have continued the jigsaw without the help of the French community where Colin had been killed. The second of the two significant breakthroughs came when Armelle Burbaud contacted me from France. Armelle's father, André Burbaud, was a young teenager in 1944 and had been present at Kerbozec on the day Colin was killed. At last, I had a link with the French. Armelle soon put me in touch with others, most notably Eliane Lebas, who, as the teenage daughter of the elderly farmer at Kerbozec, Louis Fiche, was also on the farm that day. Eliane, now in her eighties, has continued to provide me with so much information over the past few years and has shared her personal memories with me ever since. I have also been most fortunate to have the help of two

ACKNOWLEDGEMENTS

English ladies, both of whom had long settled in Brittany: Ruth Plumb and Bobbie Chinnick. I would, therefore, like to thank Ruth and Bobbie for all their help with e-mails and translations over the past few years.

Having pieced most of the jigsaw together, all that was missing was for me to go to France to visit the Guiscriff Communal Cemetery, where Colin lies buried alongside his French comrades, and to go to Kerbozec to see where Colin had spent the last moments of his life. Then, in 2012, I was delighted to receive an invitation from the Mayor of Querrien, Marcel Moysan, to attend the 68th anniversary of the battle of Kerbozec. I was fortunate to be able to travel to Querrien with four colleagues from the Royal Air Force, where we met up with Angela Weston and her daughter, Sam Gardner. During our three days in Querrien, we visited many of the places where Colin had stayed during his time in France. These included the farm at Lopers, where Colin had first established contact with the *Maquis*; the farm at Kerbozec, where Colin and team Francis had been in hiding and where Colin was ultimately killed; the cemetery at Querrien, where Colin was first buried; and the Guiscriff Communal Cemetery, where Colin lies buried today. During the visit I was delighted to meet those who had already helped me so much – Ruth, Bobbie, Armelle and Eliane – and to meet many others, including Louis Kervédou (who had been at the farm at Lopers the day Colin first arrived) and Denise Le Moine (whose father sheltered Francis at his farm at Fornigou); like Eliane, Louis and Denise were both teenagers in 1944 but their memories of Colin had remained as vivid as ever. I was also fortunate to meet Yves Naour (the son of the miller at the Moulin de Kerlévéné), as well as former members of the *Maquis*. They all contributed to the story in some way and I would like to thank, in particular, Guy Savin, George Hotte and Jean Brezulier for taking the time to share their experiences with me. I have since received further information from Gérard Flatrès and Marc le Meur; Gérard is a friend of Guy Savin and Marc's grandfather, Louis Le Meur, was a former *maquisard*.

Everywhere we went during our stay in France the organisation and hospitality were outstanding. Not only were we hosted throughout by the mayor, Marcel Moysan, who gave up all his time to make sure our visit ran on rails, we were also made so welcome at Guiscriff, so I must also say a particular thank you to Renée Courtel, the Mayor of Guiscriff, and her *adjoint*, Claudine le Scouarnec. My memories of the most generous hospitality of Marcel and the people of Querrien will live with me forever and I hope I have remembered everyone who made the visit truly unforgettable; if not then I can only apologise. I also hope that I have been correct in my understanding of the French language and that my spelling of French words is correct; any errors are purely down to my poor grasp of the French language. I would also like to thank Marcel Moysan, once again, for agreeing to write a few words at the front of the book. As the Mayor of Querrien, Marcel has done so much to ensure that the *Major Anglais* has never been forgotten and I am truly thankful for all that he has done.

Finally, I would like to thank the staff at The National Archives, particularly Paul Johnson at the image library, and to thank Michael Leventhal and Kate Baker at Frontline for their help in this publication. Without Michael's support, this story would have remained hidden in a folder somewhere in my study and would never have been given the chance to be told. That would have been such a shame.

Introduction

IT WAS A BEAUTIFUL Saturday morning at Kerbozec, a remote farm in western Brittany. As I looked down the gentle slope across the farmer's field, it presented a scene of peace and tranquillity. Behind me I could hear the sound of many people, a mix of war veterans and members of the local community who had gathered with dignitaries and invited guests to remember the events of many years before. Now, with the ceremony over, they were enjoying themselves in the way that only the French know how. But as the others relaxed, I pictured the scene of the early evening of 29 July 1944, exactly sixty-eight years before, when the peace and tranquillity was suddenly shattered by a raging battle.

Amongst those who died that day was Major Colin Ogden-Smith, an army officer and former commando but then operating behind enemy lines with the Special Operations Executive as the leader of a three-man Jedburgh team called Francis. Like so many other poignant stories, Colin need not have been there that day. He could have taken his chances with the Royal Artillery, the regiment in which he had been commissioned, but, in 1940, he chose instead to be amongst the first to volunteer for the newly formed commandos. His personal diary kept at that time gives a marvellous insight into his life as a commando, particularly while serving with Layforce in North Africa and Crete. In particular, the entries covering the frantic few days during the evacuation of Crete at the end of May 1941 make most interesting reading. Had he not have been amongst the last to escape from the island then he might well have survived the war. That said, rather than accept life as a prisoner of war, he might well have tried to make his escape in some other way or have fled to the hills to join one of the partisan groups that continued to harass the German occupying forces; we shall never know. Colin then joined the Small Scale Raiding Force, an elite group of men given the freedom to carry out nuisance raids across the Channel. They were pioneers of amphibious operations but few would live to see the freedom they had all fought so gallantly for. When the unit disbanded, Colin was a natural choice for the SOE's Jedburgh programme but as an instructor at the Jedburgh Training School at Milton Hall he need not have parachuted behind enemy lines. It was only because of a shortage of suitable officers that he volunteered to lead a 'Jed' team into France. It was a decision that would ultimately cost him his life.

Sixty-eight years later, as I looked down across the field at Kerbozec to where Colin had died that day, a most delightful French lady stood by me. Now in her eighties, Eliane Lebas had been sixteen years old at the time and we were standing together at the farm that had been her home that fateful day. Her elderly father, Louis Fiche, had also been killed that day, as had a brave young Frenchman, Maurice Miodon, who had died alongside Colin so that others could make their escape. The events of 29 July 1944 have lived in her memory ever since. After many years of research, I felt honoured and privileged to share that very special moment with Eliane.

The French have never forgotten Colin Ogden-Smith, the man they remember as the *Major Anglais*, and after seven years of research I am delighted to be able to tell the story of one of the bravest men to have served with both the commandos and the SOE during the Second World War. I only hope I have done Colin the justice he truly deserves.

Peter Jacobs

CHAPTER ONE

A Hand Of Steel

As THE B-24 LIBERATOR commenced its final run-in towards the drop zone, the young American aircraft dispatcher removed the wooden trapdoor and stood beside the 'Joe hole'. He beckoned Ogden-Smith forward. The fuselage was dimly lit but the sight of the tall and heavily laden British major edging his way forward was a fearsome one. The aircraft was now flying lower and lower, and through the small hole in the fuselage floor the ground could be seen rushing past; the patchwork of fields and woods, with the occasional village illuminated only by the moonlight, gave an impression of a murky grey countryside below. Alongside Ogden-Smith in the cramped fuselage of the converted American bomber was a twenty-four-year-old French lieutenant, about to return to French soil for the first time in years, and a youthful British sergeant radio operator, still only nineteen and about to experience action for the first time. Ogden-Smith made his final preparations to jump. He had been into action before: in North Africa and Crete, and during his days carrying out covert operations across the English Channel less than two years before. He knew what it felt like to be behind enemy lines. But this was going to be different – very different. It was now July 1944 and the Allies were on the offensive, but the landscape he could see below was Brittany – in the north-west corner of France and still a long way behind enemy lines, and even further from the leafy suburbs of south London where his life had begun nearly thirty-four years before.

Born on 30 August 1910, Colin Malcolm Ogden-Smith was one of a generation of young men that would later be called upon, quite literally, to face a total war unleashed by Nazi Germany. His two brothers – Tony, who had been born three years earlier, and Bruce, who would be born eight years later – were also part of that same generation and all three brothers would ultimately go to war, although their experiences and the outcomes would be quite different.

Unlike so many born of the same period, it is fair to say that Ogden-Smith enjoyed a relatively comfortable upbringing in the desirable area of Addiscombe in East Croydon. His father was a fishing-tackle manufacturer and the family business had been established for fifty years, with nine branches spread across the suburbs of south London.

Unsurprisingly, the early lives of the three brothers followed a similar pattern. All three were well educated at the Whitgift School, the oldest school in Croydon, although their age spread meant they were never all there at the same time. They all enjoyed similar outdoor pursuits – which centred on the family's fishing tackle business but also included shooting, riding and sailing – and all three were territorial soldiers in the same company of the Infantry Battalion of the Honourable Artillery Company, the most prestigious regiment in the British Army.

By the late 1930s Ogden-Smith was a factory manager and a director of the family business. He was well travelled for the time, as his work had taken him to America and across Europe – mostly to France, where he had spent many months of his life. Although he had worked in the family business since leaving school at the age of seventeen, his interest in the military was well substantiated and stemmed back to his days at school. As a young boy he had attended Addiscombe College, a grand mansion built by the Honourable

3. Walter and Jean Ogden-Smith raised their family in East Croydon and ran a very successful fishing-tackle business with nine branches across the suburbs of south London. Their three sons – Tony, Colin and Bruce – would all go to war but with very different outcomes. (Angela Weston).

East India Company in the mid-nineteenth century to train officers for the Indian regiments. Then, at Whitgift, the school's officer training corps had provided him with military-based training that included activities such as shooting, field craft and night exercises, carried out in after-school hours and at weekends. This had given him the opportunity during his early teenage years to develop his personal qualities and the leadership skills that would stand him well in later life. Having left school, he did not hesitate to follow his older brother into the HAC, where he spent the next twelve years working his way up to the rank of lance-sergeant and demonstrating his potential for further advancement. In particular, he excelled in shooting and competed in many competitions during the 1930s, representing both his unit and the London District.

By the time Hitler's forces invaded Poland in September 1939, triggering the start of the Second World War, Ogden-Smith had left the family business and was a second lieutenant in the Royal Artillery, serving with 274 Battery, 86th (HAC) Heavy Anti-

Aircraft Regiment. He was now twenty-nine years old and much had changed in the past few years. He had met and married a local girl, Wendy Moore, and the couple were about to celebrate their first wedding anniversary at their family home in the village of Balcombe, West Sussex.

The opening months of the war did not turn out at all how Ogden-Smith might have imagined, with a lengthy period of relative inactivity on either side of the Channel. The three brothers had now gone their separate ways. Tony had initially been commissioned into the Sherwood Foresters but then transferred into the Green Howards while Bruce chose to enlist into the East Surreys. It proved to be a period of frustration for Ogden-Smith. He even managed to attend a training course at the School of Anti-Aircraft Defence at Old

4. Ogden-Smith and Wendy, 17 September 1938. The couple married in St James, London, after which they set up home in West Sussex. (Angela Weston).

Castle Head at Manorbier in Pembrokeshire, Wales, where, when the weather allowed, he was able to fire at targets being towed by aircraft flying over the Bristol Channel. The appalling weather and extreme remoteness made him feel that the war was a million miles away.

Fortunately, though, things were soon to change. Hitler's invasion of France and the Low Countries in May 1940 brought a sudden and dramatic end to the period known as the Phoney War. Until that point priority in Britain had rightly been given to the nation's defence rather than carrying out offensive operations across the Channel, but the subsequent evacuation from the beaches of Dunkirk led to Britain's prime minister, Winston Churchill, deciding to take the war to the enemy. Because Britain had no special forces at that time he proposed the formation of a new organisation, made up of volunteers, to carry out offensive action against the enemy's extended and quite vulnerable coastline in Europe. Churchill gave the new organisation the name Commandos, taken from his days as a war reporter in the Boer War when he had witnessed for himself the significant damage and losses inflicted on the British Army by the Boer's irregular forces, known as 'commandos'.

The first commando-recruiting signals, calling for volunteers prepared to undertake special service of a hazardous nature as part of special force mobile operations, started to arrive at army camps all across the country from the end of June and appeared in regimental orders throughout July. This was just what Ogden-Smith needed. The combination of his frustrations that had built during the Phoney War and his personal desire to do something more challenging than to be a London-based artillery officer, led to him being amongst the first to volunteer. He saw this opportunity as a way of escaping all the things that he found infuriating and, at times, disheartening in the army and it would give him the chance to do something new that would hopefully lead him to operations sooner rather than later.

Ogden-Smith was one of 2,000 volunteers. They came from all parts of the army, ranging from experienced regulars with previous active service in India and Palestine to former territorial soldiers and young men with little experience of the army at all. But they were all fit young men and keen on adventure. Each commando unit was to consist of a headquarters plus ten troops of fifty men each, although this would later be revised to six troops of sixty-five men. The commanding officers were given the freedom to pick their own troop commanders, who, in turn, were given a free hand in picking two subalterns as their section leaders; the subalterns, in turn, would pick their own twenty-five men from amongst the volunteers. The concept was quite simple. If things were ever to go wrong then the officers would have no one to blame but themselves and so selection of the right individuals was crucial; if their men made mistakes in training then there would be no punishments as such as there would be plenty of volunteers ready to take their place.

Selection of the officers was done by interview, with reliability, intelligence and composure being amongst the key selection criteria. Ogden-Smith was delighted to be selected for training and was allocated to the newly formed No 7 Commando, headquartered at Felixstowe on the coast of Suffolk and currently in the process of forming at several locations across eastern England from the volunteers of the army's Eastern Command.

Commando units were expected to be able to conduct irregular warfare, using hit-and-run tactics, and were expected to operate independently for at least twenty-four hours. Training was to be the toughest in the army and designed to produce a self-reliant and highly motivated commando. The men were expected to be fitter than any of their army colleagues and mature enough to cope in any situation that a commando might ever find himself in, both physically and mentally. Life was hard and every man was expected to be able to look after himself. If men were not up to the standard required then the commanding officer had the authority to have the individual returned to his original unit.

The structure of the commandos was different to that of the rest of the army. There were no support staffs, such as administrative personnel or cooks, and so each man was responsible for his own billeting and food, and was given a ration card and a daily subsistence allowance to find his own accommodation and to cover the cost of his food. For the officers the daily allowance above the normal rate of pay was just over thirteen shillings per day, regardless of rank, with the other ranks receiving about half that. To spread their allowance several men would share a room at a local house on a bed-and-breakfast arrangement. This way of life would be the norm when under routine training at home, although the commando units would move to service establishments or on board ships when preparing for deployment or an operation overseas.

There was a sense of urgency for commando operations to commence and so Combined Operations was formed under the command of Sir Roger Keyes, with responsibility for the development of ideas and equipment, and for the planning of operations to harass the enemy in any way possible. The new commando units were amalgamated into one Special Service Brigade of three battalions under the command of Brigadier Charles Haydon with No 7 Commando becoming No 2 Company of No 3 Special Service Battalion, while No 4 Commando became No 1 Company.

As 1940 began to draw to a close, and with Britain having secured its survival for another year at least, the new commando units started assembling at towns along the west coast of Scotland in preparation for the final part of their training. Landing craft had been made available and the men were to undergo specialist training on the troop-carrying ships adapted for assault landings, known as 'Landing Ship, Infantry', or LSI, and the purpose-built 'Landing Craft, Assault' (LCA).

It was early evening of 4 December when Ogden-Smith arrived in Girvan in South Ayrshire on the west coast of Scotland. On any other day its beaches and cliffs overlooking the entrance of the Firth of Clyde would have made a wonderful view but on this particular night it was dark and miserable. He was tired and hungry. It had already been a long journey from London and now there was no one there to meet him.

It was on this day in Scotland that Ogden-Smith decided to record his activities in a diary – not in a proper daily or weekly diary as such, but he kept his record of events in a small pocket-size Walker's ring-leaf notebook that he must have been carrying on him at the time. It was the start of a diary that he would maintain throughout his time with the commandos. Most entries were brief, and always in very small writing to maximise the number of words on a page. The opening entry simply recorded:

Arrived Girvan about 7.00 p.m. No arrangements to meet!

The diary entry then went on to describe how Ogden-Smith made his way to the old church hall as instructed, where he was pleased to meet up with another newcomer, a captain formerly of the Gloucesters, and the two men were soon driven down the coast to where they were to be accommodated at Ballantrae. Fortunately after such a long day already, the drive did not take long and as they pulled up outside the King's Arms Hotel, Ogden-Smith was pleasantly surprised. From what he could see, Ballantrae was an attractive coastal village and the accommodation was better than he had expected. The hotel was small but it had a warm and friendly atmosphere.

That evening he was introduced to two others staying at the hotel. One was a young second lieutenant called Flood, who would become the adjutant, and the other was an older officer, Charles Vaughan, a captain who had fought as a young soldier in the First World War. Vaughan had formerly served as a regimental sergeant major in the Coldstream Guards and knew he would be considered too old for active operations and so he had volunteered for the commandos for administrative duties.

Later that evening they were all joined by their new commanding officer, Dudley Lister, a lieutenant colonel formerly of the East Kent Regiment. Lister had been awarded a Military Cross during the First World War and had set up No 7 Commando but was now to command No 3 Special Service Battalion. During their conversation Ogden-Smith learned that the battalion had been officially formed three weeks earlier and that its headquarters, along with No 2 Company, had been set up at Girvan, while No 1 Company was further north at Troon. The atmosphere was very much one of excitement as the men spent the rest of the evening getting to know each other and speculating about what might lay ahead.

The following day Ogden-Smith was interviewed again and told he was to be allocated to No 2 Platoon, part of B Troop and located at Girvan. Most of the day was then spent being issued with his kit, although he and some of the others did find time to do some local climbing before darkness fell. The next two days were spent picking up supplies from No 1 Company's base at Troon and visiting the commando headquarters at Stirling before returning to Girvan. There were still more arrivals and it was now that he met up for the first time with his company commander, Major Felix Colvin, and the troop commander of A Troop, Captain Ken Wylie.

With everyone having arrived, the strength of the battalion reached sixty-four officers and 847 other ranks. On 8 December Ogden-Smith moved to Gourock, just to the west of Glasgow, where he first met up with his troop leader, Captain Gus March-Phillipps, and a fellow subaltern in B Troop, Lieutenant Geoffrey Appleyard. The two men clearly knew each other well and it soon came out in conversation they had first met while taking cover in sand dunes on an evacuation beach at Dunkirk. Both had subsequently volunteered for the commandos and when March-Phillipps was appointed as a troop leader, he had not hesitated in selecting Appleyard to lead one of his sections.

Gus March-Phillipps, simply known to his men as Gus, was considered by many to be the archetypal English hero. He was thirty-two years old, extremely intelligent, literary-minded, an all-round sportsman and intensely fit. He was also charismatic and had the looks that women simply loved. Like Ogden-Smith, he was a former artillery officer and had also become disillusioned by conventional military life. He wanted to make his own personal contribution to the war effort and felt the commandos would now give him that opportunity.

Known to his friends as Apple, Geoffrey Appleyard had volunteered for the commandos from the Royal Army Service Corps. He looked much younger than his twenty-four years. Born and raised in Yorkshire, he was the son of a successful motor trade entrepreneur and had enjoyed the benefits of a privileged background. He was a graduate of Caius College, Cambridge with a first in engineering, he was a skiing blue and competitor at international level, as well as excelling as an oarsman and being the college's captain of boats.

Ogden-Smith's diary entry for 8 December recorded his first meeting with March-Phillipps and Appleyard:

> *Posted to B Troop. Captain March-Phillipps (Gus) a very fine chap I think. Lieutenant Appleyard is my opposite number, also good. They made me very welcome.*

Although he could not possibly have known at the time, March-Phillipps and Appleyard would have a huge influence on Ogden-Smith and would shape the rest of his war. If first impressions are ever anything to go by then the signs were good from the start and an instant friendship was formed. Ogden-Smith took an instant liking to both. Appleyard, in particular, would become a very close friend, not only because they were subalterns together and serving in the same troop but also because they shared so much in common and were both very similar in character.

The following day the men were up early to make the short distance to the docks at Greenock where they boarded their LSI, HMS *Glengyle*, for the first time. The 10,000-ton *Glengyle* had only recently entered service. She had been built for the Glen Line as a fast passenger-carrying cargo ship and was originally intended for the Far East trade route. Capable of a speed of eighteen knots, she had been identified as suitable for service as a large landing ship for the infantry and, after modification, the ship was capable of carrying twelve LCAs and one LCM (Landing Craft, Mechanised) plus 700 troops and equipment. Ogden-Smith's description of the *Glengyle* seemed to sum up the feeling amongst his colleagues:

She is a queer tub. Some of the mess decks are not at all good. But we're all set for a real show. My hammock is slung very close to others and we have twenty-five in this room.

With the other two battalions of the Special Service Brigade embarked in their own ships – No 4 Battalion on board the *Glenroy*, one of the *Glengyle*'s three sister ships, and No 2 Battalion embarked in HMS *Royal Scotsman*, a former passenger ship requisitioned by the Admiralty as another LSI – the three ships set sail for the Isle of Arran early the following day. It was breezy and the Firth of Clyde produced quite a swell. Conditions on board were unfamiliar to most and so the men had to adapt to their new surroundings while being subjected to the routines of the Royal Navy. During the morning the men carried out physical training on board, after which there were a number of lectures. Later in the day the men were briefed by Dudley Lister on the likelihood of an operation in the near future, although there were no details of where or when.

What the men on board the ships did not know at the time was that back at the headquarters of Combined Operations, Sir Roger Keyes had proposed that the commandos capture an island in the Mediterranean as a supplementary base to Malta, and had identified the island of Pantelleria, a small island off Sicily, as a potential target. The idea was further worked up under Operation Workshop and training was to take place on Arran.

By the end of their first day at sea the *Glengyle* had anchored in Lamlash Bay on the east coast of Arran. The following morning the men made their way down the ladders and into the landing craft for the first time. For the next couple of days the commandos trained in amphibious warfare and exercised on Arran and Holy Isle, a small island in Lamlash Bay. The terrain was rugged, the weather wintry, and the water temperature in the lochs was bitterly cold but the men trained hard together. It proved an ideal training environment. The commandos were becoming increasingly hardened towards the harsh conditions, and in addition to training for more familiar small-scale raids the brigade also began preparations for larger operations.

With an immense ability to motivate his men and to forge a team in which rank played little part, March-Phillipps was a quite extraordinary character and an exceptional leader. Some would have found him exasperating and could never have served with him but the men under his command gave their complete loyalty and trust, with each man believing he played a vital role. Because March-Phillipps was intensely fit he would often take an instant dislike to anyone carrying just an ounce too much weight. He could also be impatient with anyone who dithered or demonstrated any kind of slackness and his emphasis was always to get on quickly with the task and to do it to the highest standard. More often than not he would lead his men across the most difficult terrain and then scale the heights by the most challenging route in order to achieve the task, but his leadership soon won the admiration of his men; Ogden-Smith admired and respected him from the start. Much of this was new to Ogden-Smith but he and Appleyard both learned so much from March-Phillipps, who, above all, would prove to be exceptionally brave.

The weather deteriorated over the next few days as a gale raged across the area, making amphibious training almost impossible, and so the *Glengyle* moved further north to Brodick Bay. Now located in a more sheltered position, the commandos could continue with their landing craft training. Much of their training was conducted at night and Ogden-Smith soon enough realised just what a challenge that could present after the commandos were landed on the wrong beaches during one night exercise.

Having briefly returned to Greenock to take on supplies, the ships then sailed back to Arran. Rumours on board were now rife that something big was soon to happen, possibly within the next two to three weeks, and the level of excitement increased on 19 December when news filtered through that Sir Roger Keyes was about to board the ship to address the battalion. However, Keyes had simply come to meet the men and see how training was progressing; he quickly had to dispel the rumour that an operation was imminent. The news came as a disappointment to the commandos and so, for the time being at least, the men prepared for more training.

The *Glengyle* sailed round the coast to Blackwaterfoot on the western side of Arran, where Lister could set up his headquarters, with No 1 Company located at nearby Shiskine and No 2 Company on the northern coast at Lochranza. It was midday on 21 December when Ogden-Smith finally disembarked the *Glengyle* and after wandering north up the coast for what seemed like several hours he was one of seven officers who set up accommodation with their men at the Lochranza Hotel. In one of many letters home to his parents, which were later published by Geoffrey's father after the war,[1] Appleyard wrote:

> *Billets in houses had been arranged for the seven of us (all the other officers have gone into billets) but we thought it would be more fun to live with our troops and would also cheer them up over Christmas and prevent them feeling that they hadn't been given a square deal. Gus and Colin are, of course, two of the seven. Actually we have a lot of fun.*

The hotel had clearly been abandoned for the winter and with the exception of a table and a few chairs there was no other furniture to be found. The weather had turned bitterly cold and there was no heating and no lighting, and there was no food to be found. Fortunately most of the rooms had fireplaces and so the men gathered as much wood as they could carry. It was not long before fires were raging and the men had also managed to buy some oil lamps and candles, and had found some army rations to eat. Ogden-Smith had always enjoyed cooking and managed to create something special from their combined rations.

Eventually the men could settle down for the night. They spread out across the hotel with anything between five and twenty men per room and using blankets to lie on, with more blankets on top, and using their clothes as a pillow. It was the best they could do. Surprisingly, Ogden-Smith had a good night's sleep but others did not and so there were a few disgruntled comments the following morning. March-Phillipps and Appleyard promptly went out for a walk and some considerable time later returned having purchased a boat. It was to be the troop's boat and they had bought it from an ex-fisherman who was now in the navy.

By now Ogden-Smith had got to know March-Phillipps and Appleyard well enough to know that both loved boats. He also knew just how impulsive they could both be and so an impromptu decision such as this did not take him totally by surprise, although some of the others were left rather bemused. They were about to deploy overseas on operations, which could happen any day, and their troop leader had decided to buy a boat! What were they meant to do, take it with them?

The boat, called *I'm Alone*, had cost £35. It was five and a half tons, yawl-rigged and 32 ft long with a 15 hp paraffin engine. Ogden-Smith was one of those who contributed towards the cost and so he now had a £1 share in a boat. The intent was to use *I'm Alone* to teach the men how to sail and navigate and generally to be comfortable in a nautical environment, although Ogden-Smith would later realise there was more behind the idea than might have first appeared. Because it was only a matter of time before the commandos would be called away, March-Phillipps had made provision for *I'm Alone* to be taken to Girvan, where some friends of his would look after it until the commandos returned. He even had plans for after the war as he and Appleyard had already discussed buying out the shares and taking *I'm Alone* on numerous voyages.

The acquisition of *I'm Alone* gave the troop a new interest and it would keep them busy over the Christmas period. The following day the men were busy working on the boat – caulking seams, fitting a new mast (which they made from a pine tree), making a second cabin, fixing lighting and overhauling the engine – with a view to having her ready to go to sea on Christmas Day.

Meanwhile, the hotel had proved far from ideal and so on Christmas Eve the officers moved into a house called Westwood. Westwood was much smaller than what they had been used to but it was furnished and comfortable; Ogden-Smith and Appleyard were to share a room. After moving in their equipment and belongings they took their men on a long hike over the hills. Although the wind felt cold, the weather was relatively mild for the time of year, the scenery was beautiful and the wildlife spectacular.

Even though Ogden-Smith had been in Scotland for a short period of time, he had fitted in very well with his fellow officers, particularly with Appleyard. In a letter home, Appleyard wrote:[2]

Colin is proving to fit in with March-Phillipps and me extremely well. I like him immensely. Jolly good cook, too, which may partly explain our enthusiasm for him. But I am just beginning to wonder if I didn't eat rather too much of his excellent Welsh rarebit for supper.

The men made every effort to make it feel like Christmas. Ogden-Smith and Appleyard adorned their room with cards spread across the mantelpiece and holly on the walls; even the dying embers in the grate added to the effect. Christmas Day was spent giving out food to their men before picking holly for the dining room and making an alcoholic concoction that somehow resembled a rum punch. They all made the best of the circumstances and marked the day as traditionally as possible with a full dinner of turkey and Christmas pudding followed by whisky and brandy, chocolates and cigarettes.

The following days were spent back on the hills and listening to briefings. The planned Christmas Day voyage on *I'm Alone* had not been possible but there was time to work on the boat during the days after and they eventually put to sea a few days later. The men were able to take *I'm Alone* out to sea on a few occasions before the New Year. The weather had now turned wet and extremely windy but it was nonetheless great fun. Not only did they do all the things they had planned to do, such as teaching the men how to navigate at sea and general seamanship, they also developed tactics and techniques of how to get men ashore quickly.

By now March-Phillipps, Appleyard, Ogden-Smith and others were immersed in the idea of amphibious warfare and they exchanged ideas about how they could use a small boat, such as *I'm Alone*, to take the war to the enemy by conducting small-scale raids on enemy positions. Not only would such raids mean the enemy would have to divert vital resources to defend certain key positions but the effect it would have on the enemy psyche could be immense. This, they believed, was what combined operations and being commandos was all about. These were early and important days in developing the concept of conducting amphibious warfare using small groups of men and an inconspicuous boat – others more senior would have to be convinced, but the ideas being discussed by this small group of men would later come to fruition.

Things were now looking up, particularly when, early in January, Lister was informed that a planned operation was imminent and that his men were to be given two weeks' embarkation leave before leaving Scotland for somewhere overseas. At last Lister could give his men some more positive news, as he had sensed that the cancellation of the previous operation had impacted on their morale.

During the long journey south to London, Ogden-Smith was able to reflect on the past few weeks. The operation he had yearned for was soon to take place and he was delighted with the way things had gone, and with the people he was now with. In particular, he had got to know March-Phillipps and Appleyard very well, and he realised these two men were quite special. As he neared home, though, his thoughts were no longer of amphibious operations, or any other kind of operations for that matter.

The two weeks of leave soon passed and before he knew it Ogden-Smith was back at Gourock and then back on the *Glengyle*, but he had returned from leave to discover that neither March-Phillipps nor Appleyard were on board – in fact they were nowhere to be seen. Understandably, he was disappointed as he had looked forward to being reunited with both of them more than any of the others. It would be sometime before he found out the reason for their absence but, for now, he assumed this was how life would be in the commandos: men would come and go. So he simply pushed his memories of *I'm Alone* and their ideas of specialist amphibious warfare to the back of his mind.

It was now 28 January and the following morning the *Glengyle* sailed back to Lamlash Bay where it anchored so that Lister could disembark with his battalion headquarters and most of No 1 Company. Ogden-Smith remained on board, as did the rest of No 2 Company, and they were now joined by a handful of officers and nearly a hundred men from No 1 Company to bring their unit up to full combat strength. The following day was spent on board. There was seemingly nothing to do and there was still no sign of March-Phillipps or Appleyard.

The organisation of the commandos now changed once more. The idea of special service battalions had proved too unwieldy and had not worked well and so it was to be back to the original commando titles with No 2 Company reverting to its original title of No 7 Commando. This reverse was greeted as good news. The commandos clearly preferred their original titles as it gave them a much stronger feeling of identity.

Finally Appleyard got in touch: he and March-Phillipps were destined for operations elsewhere with another organisation. Although Ogden-Smith felt disappointed that they would not be sailing on the *Glengyle* as part of the forthcoming operation with No 7 Commando, he was nonetheless pleased to have made contact with Apple before he sailed. The two friends wished each other well and offered their good luck to each other before they went their own ways. While they had talked of meeting up again before too long, they both knew that would depend on many things – not least, them both surviving the operations they were about to take part in. Ogden-Smith simply recorded:

Heard from Apple. He and Gus have scheme in hand but not returning.

It would be another year before he would meet up with them both again but what Ogden-Smith did not know at that time was that Gus and Apple had been identified as just the sort of men needed by the recently formed Special Operations Executive. Considered to be the fourth armed service, the SOE had been formed after the fall of France when Churchill had wanted to hit back at the enemy on mainland Europe in whatever way he could. Like commando raids, SOE operations would divert vital enemy resources to counter acts of aggression but Churchill also realised that any act of aggression, no matter how small, would help raise the morale of those under occupation. In Churchill's own words he had instructed the SOE to 'set Europe ablaze' but the new organisation was to be kept separate from existing military and intelligence organisations, and was instead required to work closely with the many resistance movements in occupied Europe.

The *Glengyle* was now within hours of sailing and, with the departure of March-Phillipps, there was discussion about who would become troop leader. There was clearly a shortage of officers in the rank of captain, or even experienced lieutenants, and so Ogden-Smith was delighted to find out that he was to be given temporary command of B Troop on promotion to the rank of lieutenant. In his diary he recorded:

Am given B Troop much to my joy but no captaincy. Put up second pip.

He would naturally have preferred the appointment to be permanent and to have been given immediate promotion to the rank of captain, thereby bypassing the rank of lieutenant altogether (such things did happen in wartime), but he was nonetheless pleased to be promoted. He was also pleased with the two subalterns placed under his command. One, Don Passmore, was formerly of the HAC and had joined the commandos from the Northamptonshire Regiment, and the other, called Ford, was from the Black Watch. Ogden-Smith had got to know them well and considered both to be most efficient and good officers; he just hoped they would prove to be as good in combat as they had been in training.

His good news of promotion was followed by more good news as the *Glengyle* was about to leave the west coast of Scotland. Sir Roger Keyes had again gone on board to address the commandos, only this time he was able to bring the men good news. The operation was now on but Keyes did not say where.

With the cancellation of Operation Workshop and a sense of decreasing morale amongst the commandos, the Chiefs of Staff had decided that a major operation was needed as soon as possible and so a composite commando force was now being put together to capture the island of Rhodes. The force was to be made up of Nos 7, 8 and 11 Commandos plus one troop of No 3 Commando. The combined force, totalling nearly 2,000 men, was to be commanded by Lieutenant Colonel Robert Laycock of No 8 Commando, known to his men as 'Lucky Laycock'. The force was to be known as Z Force (to conceal its content) but it would soon become known as Layforce, named after its commander.

With No 7 Commando embarked in *Glengyle*, No 8 Commando in *Glenroy* and the men of No 11 Commando split between the two ships, the commandos prepared to set sail. There was time for one last brief from the brigade commander, Brigadier Charles Haydon. Again, there were no clues as to their destination but the commandos had been guessing for some time. The training endured during the past few weeks suggested that the capture of an island seemed most probable and the Mediterranean, as the only real active theatre of operations for such a force, seemed the most likely destination. Finally, it was time to go. Late in the evening of 31 January 1941 the *Glengyle* slipped down the Firth of Clyde and out into the Atlantic.

CHAPTER TWO

Layforce

B Y THE TIME OGDEN-SMITH woke the following morning, the *Glengyle* was already way out into the Atlantic. Unfortunately they had sailed into a storm and so he decided to go up on deck. The sea was quite rough, making a number of the men ill, but, surprisingly to him, he did not feel too bad; just as long as he could stay up on deck.

Initially, the *Glengyle* and *Glenroy*, and their escort, the cruiser HMS *Kenya*, formed part of a large convoy heading for the United States. Having got a long way across the Atlantic, almost as far as the North American continent, they left the large convoy and headed back towards the west coast of Africa. Their eventual destination was to be Egypt but rather than run the gauntlet of the Mediterranean, the sea transit would take them the longer route around the Cape of South Africa and so they would not arrive for several weeks.

The weather gradually improved over the next few days and the sea became much calmer, and after a week the men were well into the routine of life onboard ship. The time had given Ogden-Smith a chance to get to know the new officers that had been transferred from No 1 Company before the ship sailed from Arran. One was Peter Wand-Tetley. As a new and very junior addition to the unit, Wand-Tetley had been given something of a supernumerary position as Felix Colvin's liaison officer. Although Wand-Tetley was ten years younger than Ogden-Smith, it was the start of a good friendship and both men would follow very similar paths, focused on special operations, in the years ahead.

After ten days at sea the *Glengyle* arrived at Freetown. For Ogden-Smith it was his first view of Africa. With its beautiful small bays on the northern part of the town, the coastline and palm trees were much what he had expected but he was surprised by the size of the town and the military defences that had been put in place. It was only intended to be a short replenishment stop but the harbour was full and the men were not allowed to go ashore. They spent their time instead up on deck taking in the spectacular sight of seventy ships in the harbour.

The *Glengyle* and *Glenroy* continued their journey the following morning, now escorted by the heavy cruiser HMS *Dorsetshire* and three destroyers. It had become very hot and conditions on board were far less comfortable. Ogden-Smith, like many others, chose to sleep up on deck rather than down below. The following day, 12 February, witnessed much fun on board as the ships crossed the equator. Most of the men were crossing the equator for the first time and for a while they could forget the war as they enjoyed the traditional equator-crossing ceremony featuring the Ruler of the Raging Main, King Neptune, with his wife being impressively played by the battalion's administrative officer, Major Brian Ashford-Russell.

The long passage at sea had given Colvin the chance to reorganise his unit and Ogden-Smith's short period in temporary command of B Troop came to an end when Derek Thirkell-White was given command of the troop. Although Ogden-Smith was pleased to be told that he was to remain with B Troop, the news came as a great disappointment to him. He had known his appointment as troop leader was only a temporary one and so the news was not entirely unexpected. During their chat together, Colvin told Ogden-Smith that he was a lot like March-Phillipps – whether that was a good thing in the eyes of Colvin or not was not made clear but to Ogden-Smith it came as a great compliment.

The following day the *Glengyle* docked at Cape Town. It was now 19 February and at last the men could get ashore after nearly three weeks at sea. There was a warm welcome for the commandos during the customary route march into the city before Ogden-Smith spent the afternoon relaxing in the Waldorf Hotel. Then in the evening he took the cable car up Table Mountain. It was dark when he arrived at the top but the sight of the myriad of lights some 3,500 feet below was quite spectacular. The war again seemed a million miles away.

There was more shore leave the following day before the *Glengyle* was on its way once more. Escorting ships came and went, as did rumours of enemy submarines and warships, but slowly the *Glengyle* made its way around the Cape and into the Indian Ocean and then northwards up the east coast of Africa. Ogden-Smith spent the days at sea learning Morse code, his teacher being one of the Royal Air Force officers on board.

Having made its way up the Gulf of Aden and the Red Sea, the *Glengyle* entered the Gulf of Suez, two weeks after leaving Cape Town. They arrived at Suez on 7 March but the men were not allowed to go ashore. This gave Ogden-Smith the chance to catch up on his fishing. Finally, on 11 March, they disembarked for the tented camp at Geneifa, some twenty miles to the north of Suez.

Ogden-Smith had arrived in Egypt at a time when Rommel's formidable Afrika Korps was driving the British back in the Western Desert. Layforce was allocated to the 6th Infantry Division but the three commando units were to lose their commando titles once again and were now to be renamed for a second time. No 7 Commando became A Battalion of the 6th Division, No 8 Commando became B Battalion and No 11 Commando became C Battalion. D Battalion was formed by the amalgamation of Nos 50 and 52 Commandos, already based in the Middle East and made up from volunteers in Egypt and Palestine. Laycock was promoted to colonel as his force now totalled over 2,200 men. In turn, Colvin was promoted to lieutenant colonel with A Battalion consisting of thirty-six officers and 540 men. The other three battalions were each of similar size and commanded by Dermot Daly, Dick Pedder and George Young respectively.

The first month in Egypt was spent between Geneifa and Kabrit where a combined training centre had been set up. Situated on the Little Bitter Lake and surrounded by barren desert and rocky plains, Kabrit was ideal for training. The men were able to carry out amphibious training on the lake while conducting more rugged training on land in the surrounding area. Away from the hard training in intense heat, there was time for relaxing and recreation, during which Ogden-Smith, Passmore and Wand-Tetley managed to sample the delights of Suez, Tewfik and Cairo, including a visit to the pyramids.

5. Ogden-Smith relaxing in Alexandria in 1941, soon after his arrival with Layforce. (Charmian Musgrove).

The idea of capturing Rhodes was brought to a sudden end when the Germans invaded Greece on 6 April 1941. The role of Layforce was now changed to one of conducting raids behind enemy lines along the North African coast. The commandos were no longer part of 6th Division but were placed under XIII Corps instead.

The disappointing news of the cancelled operation to Rhodes soon turned to excitement as Ogden-Smith and the men of A Battalion were about to become the first of Layforce to see action. After travelling to Ismailia on the west bank of the Suez Canal, the men boarded the *Glengyle* once more. Then, after a few days of shore leave in Port Said, Ogden-Smith felt that an operation was imminent. On 13 April, Easter Sunday, he recorded:

Communion and church on board. Leave cancelled at 11.00 a.m. Let us hope that we shall be of use soon with all the bad news in Greece.

The following day the *Glengyle* sailed to Alexandria. During the night of 15 April, the *Glengyle* slipped away from the safety of Alexandria and headed out to sea. The first Ogden-Smith knew about the raid was the following morning after he awoke to find the ship had already left port. The men were issued with weapons and ammunition. There was no time to think about the fact they were going into action for the first time. This was it, the moment he and his men had trained so hard for. He found out their destination was Bardia.

The picturesque Mediterranean seaport of Bardia lies on the northern coastline of Libya some 500 miles to the west of Suez and about fifty miles east of the strategically important port of Tobruk. During the early part of the Second World War it had been an Italian fortification but the town had been taken by the Allies during Operation Compass in early January 1941. Bardia had then been retaken by the Axis powers during a major offensive by Rommel in Cyrenaica and the Allies were now putting together a plan to carry out a raid on the port to disrupt the enemy's lines of communication and to cause as much damage as possible. Layforce was considered ideal for such an operation and success would announce their arrival in the region. Furthermore, the longer-term effect would be to divert vital German resources away from other strategic locations, such as Sollum and Tobruk, in order to defend Bardia.

Intelligence had led the commandos to believe that Bardia was an important enemy headquarters and defended by up to 2,000 Italians. A plan was put in place involving simultaneous landings on four beaches by two of the battalions. The beach furthest to the north, designated A Beach, was two miles from the town and on the far side of a headland, close to an army barracks and near to a main road junction. Also to the north was B Beach, set in a small inlet and the closest beach to the town. The other two beaches were situated to the south of Bardia: C Beach was in a small inlet off a bay and close to a bridge crossing the river entering the bay and close to a gun battery protecting the eastern approach to the town, with D Beach being about a mile to the south of the battery.

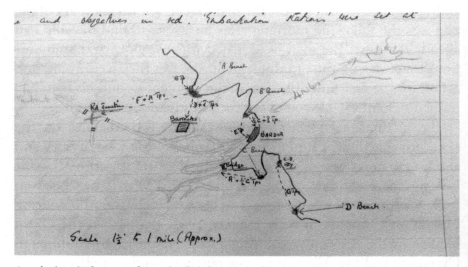

6. A sketch diagram from the Layforce war diary showing the raid on the North African coastal town of Bardia, which took place on the night of 19/20 April 1941. (National Archives WO 218/168).

The plan was for the landing force to be transported on the *Glengyle*, with an escort, and once at the designated release point to go ashore in a number of landing craft. The force was to be supported by a Royal Navy submarine, HMS *Triumph*, with a canoe section on board; they would paddle from the submarine and provide navigation lights to mark the approaches to the beaches. The whole raid was planned to be conducted during the night, with the raiders spending just a couple of hours ashore, so that the *Glengyle* could be on its way back to port before first light.

Ogden-Smith and his men went through everything one last time, but when the *Glengyle* was only fifteen miles from the drop-off point the operation was cancelled. A strong easterly wind had meant that the sea state was considered too rough. The canoe section could not disembark from the submarine and conditions along the coastline would have made it almost impossible to get back off the beaches.

The *Glengyle* turned back for Alexandria, although the high number of air-raid warnings issued by the escorting anti-aircraft cruiser did nothing to raise morale on board. Neither did the weather, as it now started to rain. Ogden-Smith's frustration is evident by his diary entry:

Owing to roughness of sea, op cancelled when only 15 miles away! Raid to be tip and run on old style. Seven or eight air raid warnings given by anti-aircraft cruiser. Only fired once at Recce plane. No bloody good.

The following lunchtime the *Glengyle* arrived back into Alexandria during the middle of a sand storm. It was now a matter of waiting. The following day Ogden-Smith was told the operation was back on and re-scheduled for the following night but this time only A Battalion would carry out the raid.

The plan was for the battalion to land seven troops, each of fifty men, on the four beaches; four troops were to land on A Beach, the main beach, and one troop was to land on each of the other three beaches, with each troop given a separate mission in and around the town. Colvin and his battalion headquarters would go ashore on A Beach as part of the third landing and Ken Wylie, his second-in-command, would go ashore on C Beach with Laycock and his staff being amongst the last to land on A Beach. Ogden-Smith was to be amongst the first to go ashore on A Beach as B Troop had been tasked to secure and hold the main beach and its surrounding area. They would then continue to hold the area while the other troops allocated to the beach, as well as Colvin's headquarters and Laycock's staff, went ashore.

During the early hours of 19 April the *Glengyle* once again slipped out of Alexandria under the cover of darkness and sailed out into the Mediterranean to meet up with her escort: a Royal Navy light cruiser and three Australian destroyers. As before, the commandos went through everything one last time. Ogden-Smith then boarded the landing craft in preparation to go ashore.

The sea swell meant there were difficulties in lowering and releasing the landing craft from the *Glengyle* and one landing craft could not be lowered at all. The operation was already behind schedule: the first landing craft should have been away at 10.15 p.m. but it was at least five minutes after that before the first ALC, with Ogden-Smith on board, headed towards the beach. Even when the landing craft were finally released, some could not locate the lights that were meant to guide them to the right beaches. The canoe section had been delayed after the submarine had come under attack from what turned out to be a friendly aircraft and had to dive to take evasive action. There were then further delays due to difficulties launching the canoes from the submarine, meaning that some of the approach lights could not be laid.

The men of B Troop were split between two ALCs and it took an hour to travel the four miles from the *Glengyle* to the beach. They managed to land on the correct beach soon after 11.30 p.m. but were now some fifteen minutes behind schedule. As with the landings on the other beaches, they had landed unopposed, and Ogden-Smith quickly took his men inland some 600 yards where they set up their defensive positions, with Don Passmore's section holding a hill to the south of the beach.

With the beach area secure, the second landing on A Beach was by F and H Troops: a hundred men in total landing in four ALCs. Their task was to set up a road block at the main road junction to prevent enemy vehicles from opposing the raid. The third landing, by D and J Troops, landed another hundred men in one LCM. They had been given the task of attacking the enemy barracks on the western side of the town. The fourth landing on the beach was by fifty men of E Troop, in two ALCs, tasked with raiding the town.

With all the commandos allocated to A Beach safely ashore, the men of B Troop were somewhat surprised to see a fifth landing made by two more ALCs. These were the seventy-one men of I Troop and half of C Troop who had been unable to locate B Beach. They had been due to land just after midnight to attack the northern part of the town but were now well behind schedule and further away than originally planned and so there was insufficient time. On C Beach the landing by the other half of C Troop and all of A Troop, another seventy men in two landing craft, had gone to plan. They had landed just after 11.30 p.m. and immediately set about destroying a pumping station and reservoir, as well as destroying a bridge and roads. On D Beach, G Troop, with just thirty-five men, had landed around the same time and went looking for the coastal battery on the peninsula to the north of their landing beach.

Rather than hang around for a couple of hours waiting for the raiding parties to return to A Beach, Ogden-Smith had been allowed to leave the beach with some of his men. They set off towards the town, where some of the enemy defences were believed to be, and to inflict more damage wherever possible. Some of the installations they were looking for were either in the wrong place or not there at all but they did manage to locate an Italian gun emplacement full of weapons and ammunition, which they immediately destroyed.

Ogden-Smith returned to A Beach before the other troops started to arrive back from their raids, but he was shocked to find that Don Passmore had been shot by an overly-eager sentry from his own section. Passmore was still alive but was clearly in a bad way. He also found one of the ALCs was ablaze: it had been damaged by another landing craft during the landings and had now been destroyed rather than leave it for the enemy.

The raiding parties started to arrive back at the beach. As it turned out, those tasked with raiding the barracks arrived to find it empty and those tasked with raiding the town found that Bardia had already been evacuated. While this was fortunate, in terms of the raid being unopposed and therefore not suffering any losses, it did come as something of a surprise. It was now 2.30 a.m. and time to get everyone away but there was a further problem with getting the engines started on one of the ALCs because of sand in the filter. After several attempts the engines started but even then the men struggled to get the landing craft away because it was overcrowded and there was a rough sea.

Having got everyone off the beach it was time for Ogden-Smith to leave. The journey back to the LSI was as bad as the run-in to the beach had been and they had great difficulty finding the *Glengyle*; it was pitch black and navigation was not easy. Eventually, after some searching, they found the ship.

As soon as he was safely back on board, Ogden-Smith could sense anxiety and could see for himself that there were many men missing. Amongst those missing were seven of his fellow officers. Furthermore, Don Passmore was fighting for his life; his chances of survival were not good. Ogden-Smith went to see how he was doing but came away feeling shattered. Before falling asleep, he summarised the raid in his diary:

At 10.20 p.m. left ship to land in four parties. Our beach same as last time. Our job to secure and hold beach for four troops. A fair swelling running making getting away from ship difficult. Light from submarine to guide us in. Safe and unopposed landing. Took main party to position about 600 yards from beach south-west. Sergeant Bond and seven went west. No opposition and subsequently found Bardia evacuated. Don's section held hill on left, i.e. south. We found old emplacements with arms, ammo and guns galore, all Italian. Returned to beach at 2.30 a.m. to find one ALC (No 3) ablaze. She had to be destroyed because she grounded having had her kedge cut by another ALC's prop. Also learned that Don had been accidentally shot by one of his own men. Great difficulty in getting the last ALC off as sea was getting rough and we were overcrowded. I held her head on for some time before getting away. A nightmare of a journey back with Thirkell nearly hysterical. Shipped green seas occasionally and could not find Glengyle which was out of position. Also engines failed at start owing to sand in filter. Aboard at about 4 a.m. One ALC missing with Jamie Kinross, Jim Milton and 39 ORs. Brian Ashford-Russell, Brummie Richards, Arsbeck Colbeck, Guy Ruggles-Brise, Wilf Royds and about 50 ORs left behind because no room in ALCs! Don fair. Shot under left eye and out at base of neck.'

Later that day Ogden-Smith visited Passmore again and came away feeling cheered slightly as it looked as if things were improving. He felt better in himself. There was still some way to go before they docked back at Alexandria and so it gave him time to reflect on his first operation. While it had felt good to finally be in action, the night had been disappointing overall, although much had been learned. No doubt they would all discuss the raid in detail later but his thoughts were for those still missing and, of course, for his friend, Don Passmore.

The *Glengyle* arrived back at Alexandria early evening but the men were not allowed ashore. Ogden-Smith was woken the following morning to be given the sad news that Don Passmore had just died from his wounds. He was shocked. He wrote:

Awakened at 7 to be told that Don passed away at 5 this morning. A fearful blow.

Don Passmore's funeral was held that afternoon at a British cemetery behind the hospital in Alexandria. As it turned out he was the only casualty of the Bardia raid, although seventy men had been captured and taken as prisoners of war. They had not been able to find their way back to A Beach and had headed for B Beach instead only to arrive there to find there were no landing craft, as had been planned, to get them back to the *Glengyle*; the two ALCs that should have been there were the ones that had been unable to find the beach during the initial landings and had landed at A Beach instead. With no ALCs to get them away, the men were left behind. A further forty-two men had initially been listed as missing, including Jamie Kinross and Jim Milton. A faulty compass meant they had been unable to make it back to the *Glengyle* but they had managed to make it along the coast to Tobruk, which was still in Allied hands, from where they eventually made their way back to Alexandria.

Despite all this, the army's senior commanders considered the raid on Bardia a success. It was the first of its kind in the region and demonstrated to the Axis powers that the Allies were capable of carrying out small-scale raids wherever and whenever they chose. The raid did have the effect of diverting vital German resources away from other locations, particularly from Sollum and Tobruk as had been hoped, to defend Bardia against any further raids and resulted in the port's defences being strengthened.

However, to the commandos that had taken part in the raid, Bardia was not the success the senior officers felt it to be. The raid had not gone entirely to plan and there was much to learn, although they had been lucky to have found Bardia undefended – had it have been defended then things would probably have been so much worse.

No matter how much the commandos had trained beforehand, there were still problems to overcome. The weather and light conditions they had come across in North Africa were quite different to what they had experienced during training on the west coast of Scotland. Furthermore, there should have been more thought given to the withdrawal from the enemy coast and also getting back on board the ship: the *Glengyle* should have re-positioned closer to the evacuating commandos and spare landing craft should have been made available to recover any stragglers. There were also questions raised about the level of risk taken to attack what turned out to be an empty town. Was it really worth risking the LSI and a number of escorting naval surface ships as well as a submarine to support the raid? This, in turn, brought into question the validity of the intelligence in the region at the time.

Nonetheless, the commandos felt pleased to have finally taken part in an operation. They finally left the *Glengyle* the day after Don Passmore's funeral and were transported to their new camp at Sidi Bishr. Layforce was then split up, with A and D Battalions remaining at the camp while B Battalion moved to Mersa Matruh and C Battalion moved to Cyprus.

Ogden-Smith took on the difficult task of sorting out Don Passmore's equipment and personal belongings, selling off anything that was not personal to pay off any debts. It was the first time that he had lost a friend in action but it would not be the last. For the next three weeks life settled into a routine. There was talk of further raids but they seem to have been cancelled just as quickly as the idea was put forward. There were even occasions when the commandos got to the point of embarkation only to then find out the raid had been cancelled and were transported back to camp.

After a few weeks Ogden-Smith became increasingly restless. He was pleased to learn that he had been recommended for a company commander's course, although he did not know where or when it would take place, and he was also told that he would soon be promoted to captain and given a permanent troop commander's position. However, the loss of so many men at Bardia had led to a reorganisation within A Battalion, which reduced the battalion from its ten troops to eight. Further changes included promotion to the rank of captain for Jamie Kinross and Peter Wand-Tetley was given command of the section previously led by Don Passmore.

This period of relative inactivity gave the men time to talk at length and get to know each other better, particularly those in other troops. One officer who had impressed Ogden-Smith from the start was Jocelyn Nicholls, a captain and leader of G Troop. Nicholls had already demonstrated his calm, determined and resolute leadership during the Bardia raid when he led his men ashore on D Beach in quite difficult sea conditions and then succeeded in destroying coastal defences and anti-aircraft guns on the peninsula. He looked even younger than his twenty-four years and had already experienced an interesting life. Like Ogden-Smith, he had been commissioned into the Royal Artillery before the war and when hostilities broke out he was in the Fiji Islands. He had been seconded as aide-de-camp to the governor but, not wishing to miss out on hostilities, Nicholls requested a move back home and immediately volunteered for special service in Finland to fight the Russians. Having gone through arduous mountain- and ski-training, the unit was disbanded after the Finns made peace with Russia at the end of the Winter War and so his next move had been to volunteer for the commandos.

As the commandos wondered what was to happen next, increasingly worrying news started to filter in from Greece. It was only a matter of time before they would be in action once more, although when the notice to move did come on 23 May, it was all very sudden. Ogden-Smith was woken during the early hours and told to prepare to move immediately, but having gathered his kit together, he and the other commandos of A Battalion waited for further orders. Later that day he recorded:

Sudden panic at 3.15 a.m. Prepare to move immediately. Eventually got into train at Sidi Bishr at 2.30. Sat there and then came back! Glengyle considered too good a target. Half the battalion left with Lt Col Colvin at 2 o'clock for Crete. Remainder going Saturday morning. We were so loaded up we could scarcely move.

Germany's airborne invasion of the island of Crete had taken place three days earlier. Hitler knew that occupation of the island would provide him with a stronghold in the Mediterranean from where he could support Rommel's forces in North Africa. Although the island of Malta would have been a preferred option, it was considered to be far more heavily defended than Crete. The force attacking Crete consisted of some 30,000 well-equipped paratroopers and mountain troopers, plus a further 3,000 Italian troops, all supported by 1,000 aircraft.

Crete was defended by a British garrison that had been reinforced by Commonwealth and Greek forces evacuated from mainland Greece. Known as Creforce, there were more than 40,000 Allied troops on the island but at least one-quarter of them had little or no fighting capacity and those that did lacked heavy equipment. The largest airfield on the island, Maleme, was quickly overrun by the attackers and the Germans were now able to pour reinforcements into the island from mainland Europe. Meanwhile, in Egypt, the decision was made to send a small group of commandos to recapture the airfield at Maleme in an attempt to slow down the invasion. The plan was for Colvin to set off for Crete as soon as possible with No 1 Company of A Battalion and as much equipment as they could carry, while No 2 Company, which included B Troop, along with all of D Battalion and the rest of the equipment, would follow two days later.

The commandos were placed on twelve-hour notice to move but early the following morning they were given less than two hours to be ready to sail. Two troops were immediately transported to Alexandria, where they boarded a destroyer bound for Crete, but a shortage of vehicles meant that it was some time before Ogden-Smith and his colleagues from B and C Troops could travel to the docks. They finally arrived on the quayside only to find they had arrived too late and all they could do was to stand and watch the destroyer steaming out of the docks.

Having then returned to Sidi Bishr, the men of B and C Troops were left to wonder whether they would ever get away or not.

Finally, on the evening of 25 May, Ogden-Smith and his men were transported to Alexandria once again. Unbeknown to them at the time, bad weather had meant the planned landing by the advanced force on the south of the island had not been possible and so the advanced party had returned to Alexandria. Laycock had then been instructed to land his commandos on the northern part of Crete and so Colvin and his advanced party were to land at Suda Bay.

On reaching the docks for the second time, Ogden-Smith and the rest of No 2 Company were taken to a newer-looking ship, HMS *Abdiel*, a fast minelayer capable of a speed of up to forty knots and ideal for use as a fast transport ship. It would get the commandos to Crete far quicker than the *Glengyle*. There was initially more hanging around as men and equipment were loaded on board, then the following afternoon they set sail. There was time for Ogden-Smith to add to his diary:

Moved off at 8 p.m. Found HMS Abdiel waiting. After hanging about got aboard and sailed about 3 p.m. With most of D Battalion and the other half of A which had been unable to land the night before owing to rough weather.

Even when laden with stores and ammunition, *Abdiel* could still make a good thirty knots and with her escort of two destroyers, HMS *Hero* and HMAS *Nizam*, she passed through the Mediterranean the following day. The commandos had positioned themselves around the deck in case the ship came under air attack but fortunately it was a dull day with low cloud and so the transit passed without incident. Later that night they reached Suda Bay, where the commandos were quickly put ashore so that the *Abdiel* could make her escape under the cover of darkness.

The commandos had been instructed to leave their heavy equipment on board as there was no transportation available once ashore. Leaving their packs behind, Ogden-Smith and his men collected as much ammunition and food as they could manage, packing their pouches and pockets with as much as they could physically carry. Even with Brens and rifles in hand, Ogden-Smith still felt they were too lightly armed.

As he went ashore he was surprised to find there was an atmosphere of relative calm and silence, but as the commandos started to make their way towards the town of Suda he could hear firing in the distance to the west and flares were illuminating the night sky. He also noticed a number of German prisoners. It was the first time he had seen the enemy. Many were wounded and gathered in a group in preparation for being taken off the island, and it gave an initial impression that all on Crete was not that bad.

While the sight of German prisoners may have proved encouraging for the commandos, the fact was that by the time they arrived on Crete the Allied situation had deteriorated further. Any thoughts of recapturing the airfield at Maleme had disappeared, following an earlier unsuccessful attempt, which now meant that the Allied forces on the island were fighting a constant supply of fresh enemy troops. Furthermore, the commander of Creforce, Major General Bernard Freyberg, had now ordered his troops to withdraw eastwards and to make their way to the southern side of the island, from where an evacuation could take place.

Crete is elongated in shape and spans more than 150 miles from west to east but is less than forty miles across at its widest point. The island is extremely mountainous, with a high range of peaks reaching up to 8,000 feet and crossing the island from west to east, and is lavished by a number of plateaus, valleys, gorges and rivers. The planned evacuation would be carried out by the Royal Navy from Sphakia – a small fishing port on the south of the island – while the route south would take the retreating forces through the White Mountains.

The commandos were now told they were to act as a rear guard so that as much of Creforce as possible could be evacuated from the island. Laycock's plan was for the commandos to take up a defensive position to the south-east of Suda, near to where the road split from the main coastal road south towards Sphakia, and for the companies to fight a series of holding actions as they passed through each other's defensive lines to take up new positions further south.

From a strategic point of view this was not at all what commandos were intended for and tactically not what they had been trained to do. Furthermore, the rush to disembark the commandos at Suda Bay and the lack of any suitable transportation meant that not all of their ammunition and equipment had found its way ashore, and there would be little or no chance of being resupplied as they retreated south across the island.

Having joined up with the rest of the battalion to the south-east of Suda, Ogden-Smith was instructed to take his men to a position to the south-west. When he arrived, he looked around him. It was dark but he could immediately tell his position was not good. From what he could see, three subalterns had been given defensive positions ahead of him and within his own section's arc of fire, which would mean his men having to fire over or through their positions, and the headquarters staff were behind him in reserve, while D Battalion was further to the rear. He decided it was difficult to do much there and then and so decided to wait until it was daylight before adjusting their positions.

It was now the early hours of 27 May. Finally he could rest and as he did so he finished off his diary entry for the day, summarising what had happened and recording his first impressions as he had gone ashore:

Landed in Suda Bay after 11 o'clock. Very eerie. No noise at all. A few German prisoners waiting to be taken off. After a pause when we had gone on about 300 yards up to right towards Suda we heard firing and saw Verey lights etc. to west. Were eventually told to dump our packs, my fishing rod reel and flies in it! And we collected more ammunition and moved off to a position about 1 ½ miles south-west. Here Colvin gave us positions. They were like a child's ideas! We found Hutton, Flood and Jack Owen in front of us – HQ in reserve. Food of sorts had been issued and men put into some sort of positions to wait daylight when we should be able to see where we were!

The commandos took up defensive positions wherever they could. Sometimes it was relatively easy to set up defences in softer areas of terrain, such as in the olive groves, whereas elsewhere it was hard work digging trenches in what, at times, was nothing but solid rock. Ogden-Smith found a tent but barely slept. As dawn broke he took in the scene. He was concerned they were occupying a defensive position that he felt was too enclosed. They were almost trapped. The furthest the men could see was 200 yards ahead. He was far from pleased.

The situation became even more unpleasant when the first of many air raids took place during the morning – mostly by Junkers Ju 87 Stukas carrying out diving bombing attacks against their defensive positions, but also a mix of other Luftwaffe aircraft, including strafing attacks by Ju 88s and Messerschmitt Bf 110s. But the commandos were well dug in. In between the breaks from air attack, Ogden-Smith took his diary out of his pocket and added:

Dug in. Green trees and a lovely countryside with rivers etc. A grand place which soon became unpleasant because of Gerry 110, 109, 88 flying pencils and others by the score! NZ and Aussie troops soon came through and we were told we were the last position! Much firing when an enemy patrol broke through but it did not reach us. The countryside was too enclosed to see more than 100–200 yards ahead!

As the men of Creforce filed through their defensive positions, it became clear that the commandos would soon need to move and Ogden-Smith was only too pleased when the order came through during the afternoon that they would soon be moving further south. The commander of D Battalion, George Young, had identified a suitable defensive position along the Sphakia road and near the village of Babali Hani. It was where the road over the White Mountains passed through a narrow valley with a thick covering of olive groves, effectively dividing Crete in half. To get to the southern part of the island meant passing through this vital defensive position.

The Germans were now pushing hard against the defensive lines with continuous aerial attacks combined with artillery bombardments and waves of advancing mountain troops. There had only been two brief lulls in enemy air activity during the day, with the worst of the attacks occurring where A Battalion had concentrated in the hills to cover the left flank and resulting in the battalion suffering its first casualties. Many Allied troops, mainly from Australian and New Zealand units, had already passed through the defensive positions but A Battalion was now the last in the line of defence. As dusk fell at the end of their first day of fighting, two more attacks were made against their lines. Although the initial attacks were repelled, the commandos did suffer further casualties as some of the men were withdrawn further south. Ogden-Smith's diary continues:

I walked up to see A.F.H.I. (troops) lines at 2 o'clock. We were ordered to take new position in hills about 3 miles south. Thirkell-White, Palmer and Brundell came with me and we did recce and found positions. The air became alive with planes. I had to lie up in the hills until dusk. Got chaps in position now and settled down.

B Troop, along with G Troop, led by Jos Nicholls, had been ordered to stay put until well into the night, by which time the last stragglers of Creforce had passed through. They were the last two troops to move and, as Thirkell-White and one section provided a rear guard, Ogden-Smith was told to take whatever men he could muster from B Troop, along with any others who had become separated from their own troops, as quickly as possible to take up a new defensive position on the Sphakia road. It was dark as Ogden-Smith led the rest of the men eastwards along the coast road for about three miles before turning south and passing the well at Beritiana and then up Kephala Hill. Throughout the night they kept on the move and daylight had already broken by the time they reached D Battalion's new defensive position at Babali Hani.

Laycock had set up his headquarters in a house on the edge of the village and was pleased to have now been reinforced by an Australian infantry battalion and six British Matilda tanks. The terrain had made it hard going but it was a beautiful morning and the scenery was quite stunning. At any other time of his life Ogden-Smith would have enjoyed the scenery far more but for now he had to keep going as the sound of gunfire coming from the direction of A Troop in a nearby valley and the occasional German aircraft overhead were stark reminders of the position they now found themselves in. He finally allowed his men to stop for a brief rest at a river near the village of Stylos where he was able to make contact with headquarters. Ogden-Smith was instructed to continue further south to set up another defensive position. After replenishing their water bottles they moved on once more. It was already getting hot. Having passed the small village of Provarma they were ordered to set up their next defensive position at Makhairo. It was now midday and, as Ogden-Smith surveyed the area around him from his vantage point on top of a hill, his diary captured the events of the past few hours:

At 3 a.m. ordered to close on road. Sent for Corporals Parkinson, Wynne, Mycock and Cox but could not find them or make them hear. After difficult descent told to lead B Troop and others at speed on Sphakia Road. Thirkell–White and one section acting as delaying guard. After 3 miles or so turned off onto Sphakia Road and met Jos Nicholls at top of hill where there was excellent water. Already had blister through thin socks which I had changed into for rest. Have re-formed, G in front and B in rear. Set off downhill, lovely view. Aircraft about, singles only. Heard a lot of machine gun and Tommy fire in valley on our road. A [troop]) and other troops being ambushed! Instead of going in behind we were ordered to cover road and go through trees and scrub to pass ambush. This was achieved in a scattered sort of way. Found water point at lovely clear river. Some discussion as to whether we should be used for attack. Not wanted yet so moved off about 10 a.m. A long march. Stopped about 12 o'clock at a camp where we found a few remnants, change of socks, shirts etc. A few miles on were ordered to take a position on top of hill facing west. Excellent place. Aussies to be on left and G.E.C. [troops] on our right and in support. Heard that Gerry had mountain troops and would be along very shortly!

The situation was already bad but it became worse when he noticed the Australians withdrawing to the south, leaving his left flank fully exposed. The Australians had been ordered to withdraw while the commandos covered their retreat. He could now see the first signs of the German mountain battalion as it approached and was somewhat relieved when he received the orders to withdraw to a new defensive position from where he could provide support for Young's defensive line at Babali Hani.

Ogden-Smith found an excellent location for B Troop just off the road and on top of a hill facing west. Taking up a position in a wood to the side of the road, he surveyed the scene. Now alongside E and G Troops he was satisfied they could provide support to D Battalion while the stragglers of Creforce passed through. From their own position they would be able to further delay the enemy once more but it was going to be tough.

The afternoon of 28 May witnessed the fiercest fighting of the withdrawal to Sphakia. D Battalion was attacked continuously from the air before there was a concentrated attack by two battalions of enemy mountain troops. The attack started about midday and continued for the rest of the day but time and time again the commandos repelled the attacks and prevented the Germans from breaking through; every passing hour meant the retreating Allied forces were getting closer to Sphakia.

D Battalion was then forced to withdraw southwards and through Ogden-Smith's defensive position as the mortar fire intensified. They were unable to hit back as the lack of heavy weapons became increasingly evident. Ogden-Smith's diary summarises the afternoon spent under attack:

A lot of mortar fire unpleasantly near. Samuels and Hills and 14 men hit by a mortar shell. Johnnie very badly and Sam not too good. Another found shell shocked. Sniped at good but very ineffective. Mostly explosive bullets. They make a most unpleasant crack. Withdrew at 8 o'clock. Here was a mistake as Gerry saw our going and staged a fierce attack on south side. Got chaps into a trench leading to Battalion HQ.

Unable to contact Thirkell-White, Ogden-Smith took a section of men to a new position 300 yards to the north-east but they were spotted and fired on continuously: a German sniper had managed to keep the commandos within his sights. Ogden-Smith's diary records what happened next:

We were fired on all the time and sniped effectively by one sniper who just missed us. As firing increased we were joined by Tony French and his chaps. I ordered a 'Thin Red Line' defensive position with intention of defence and subsequent withdrawal.

Ogden-Smith was determined to stop the enemy advance and he knew this could well be his last heroic stand: the term 'Thin Red Line' stemming from the Crimean War when the 93rd Highlanders stood in line to repel the Russian cavalry at Balaklava.

The men were now fighting for their lives. Ammunition was getting low and so, too, was water. It was hot. Elsewhere the commandos of A Battalion were making similar stands against overwhelming odds. Wylie led a determined and spirited counterattack while Jos Nicholls delivered another fierce counter-attack against German positions established on a hill on the extreme left flank by leading his G Troop in a heroic bayonet attack that resulted in hand-to-hand and close-quarter fighting more resembling skirmishes of the Victorian era. The action of Nicholls seizing the initiative with extreme courage is captured in the following extract from the *Green Beret*:[3]

> *During the 28th, G Troop of No 7 Commando, under F R J Nicholls, delivered a fierce counterattack upon some Germans established in a hill to the extreme left flank where they were in a position to enfilade the Commando. Nicholls led his men with fixed bayonets to the top of the hill and routed the enemy without difficulty. This was the first occasion on which the Commandos had used the bayonet, and they proved once again that the German infantry soldier, though a brave and tough fighter, dislikes cold steel. 'One thing I am certain about after Crete,' said Nicholls in a letter describing this and other actions, 'is that, man for man, there is not any question as to who is the better. Although they [the Germans] had every advantage of air support etc, whenever they counterattacked or got to close quarters, which in our own case was twice, they dropped their weapons and fled before us – a very heartening sight.*

Laycock could have asked no more of his men. In any case, he was having a hard enough time of it himself. With his headquarters having been ambushed he was relieved to have with him three tanks. 'By the most fortunate chance', he later said, 'the ambush was close to the three tanks and the Germans did not see them. The enemy were about thirty yards or less away from us when my Brigade Major and I jumped into a tank and drove straight over the Germans.'[4] Laycock and his brigade major then rejoined the main body of men, presenting a strange appearance, for the tanks were still swathed in the camouflage netting with which they had been covered.[5]

Back in the hills, and just when it looked like Ogden-Smith's position would be overrun, reinforcements arrived. He suddenly saw a brief opportunity for his men to withdraw south-eastwards towards the village of Vryses. As more German reinforcements continued to arrive, the commandos were again ordered to retreat south, and, having successfully negotiated a mined bridge along the Sphakia road, Ogden-Smith and the other survivors of A Battalion reached Ammoudari. Leaving his men at a well to rest, he walked into the village and to the battalion headquarters. Meeting up with some of the other junior officers outside an undertaker's house at the end of the village, he was told that Colvin had been taken ill and that Wylie had replaced him in command of the battalion.

Having suffered significant casualties and now facing overwhelming enemy forces, Laycock felt that a further rear guard action by A Battalion alone would be futile and so decided to merge the remnants of his force into one unit. As the main body of Creforce had now reached the south coast of the island he ordered his commandos to make their way further south towards the Askifou Plain. Ogden-Smith led his men off once again. He now had twenty men left under his command and so decided to split them into two groups. The survivors of D Battalion and the other troops all started to do the same thing. There was now an element of confusion as some groups went down the valley, some made their way across country and over the hills while others stuck to the Sphakia road. Nonetheless, they were soon able to put some distance between themselves and the enemy.

The commandos were now ordered to take up a final defensive position together some three miles to the north-east of Sphakia from where the evacuation was taking place. The Royal Navy was already suffering significant losses due to the air attacks and so the window of opportunity for the evacuation of troops was restricted to just three hours during the night so that no more ships would be lost.

Approaching the evacuation area, the scene was a desperate one. 'It was pitiful to see the state and marching of some of the British soldiers,' reported an eye witness. 'Discipline seemed to have left them; they had sore feet through sweating and marching, the skin peeling off their shoulders with carrying extra ammunition or their comrades' rifles.' The commando soldiers were not in much better shape. 'Officers and men were all alike tired and hungry,' reported one sergeant, who later sacrificed his chances of evacuation in order to help two wounded comrades, 'and man's most precious liquid, water, was running short.'[6]

The commandos were exhausted and hungry, but using all their strength and ingenuity they made their way south. Having had little to eat in the last forty-eight hours, they scrounged whatever food they could and then, having commandeered some local vehicles to transport their wounded, they arrived at the specified area to set up what would be their last line of defence. Ogden-Smith had long been separated from Thirkell-White but he had managed to join up with Wylie and amongst the survivors he was pleased to see Wand-Tetley. Ogden-Smith was instructed to take his men up to a position in the hills on the eastern side of the defensive line, overlooking the port. His entry in his diary stating *we still hoped to go that night* was nothing but optimism.

The hard fighting of 28 May had proved decisive, not because there was any victory to be won but because every day had now become crucial. The evacuation of Crete had started that day and every day of delaying tactics by the commandos would enable thousands of Allied troops to be successfully evacuated from the island.

The following morning Wylie instructed Ogden-Smith to take twenty men from the survivors of each troop down into the port to see what rations and water they could scrounge and to bring as much as the men could carry back up into the hills. It had not been a good night and Ogden-Smith was exhausted. The sounds of countless Australians trying to make their way in the dark down to the evacuation area had kept all those on top of the hill awake for much of the night. Wand-Tetley went with him and as they made their way down into Sphakia they could see the chaos and confusion for themselves. They had been told earlier that if all went well they might get off the island that night, but looking at the scene in front of them they realised there was no way that was going to happen.

Having met up with a most helpful subaltern of the Army Service Corps, they found lots of rations that had been left behind on a beach during the evacuation. Ogden-Smith told the men to feed themselves and to then gather whatever they could carry. He managed to find a sausage and some potatoes. He was hungry, very hungry, but his mouth was so dry that he struggled to swallow the food, although he did enjoy sharing a cup of tea. Having eaten what they could, the commandos returned to the hills, carrying as much as they could physically manage: sausages, potatoes and water, and even some alcohol, though there was never going to be much to go round.

That night more than 6,000 Allied troops managed to get off the island. Laycock had now received orders from Freyberg to fight to the end and he was also told that Layforce would be the last troops to be evacuated. It was a desperate situation. Ogden-Smith knew the rate of evacuation was reducing considerably and the continuous German attacks, from both the air and on the ground, suggested it would only be a matter of time before they were overwhelmed. He knew there would be little chance of getting everyone away.

The remnants of A Battalion were reorganised into two troops of fifty men each. What was left of Layforce maintained their defence positions in the hills overlooking Sphakia and for the next twenty-four hours they defended their line as the evacuation continued, ship by ship. Ogden-Smith volunteered to take a party of men to see if any more food could be found. They walked for a few miles and did have some success at a local village and took back to the hills as much as they could carry.

By the time darkness fell on 31 May some 12,000 Allied troops had been evacuated off the island, although the commandos had now almost given up any hope of getting off Crete. Most worrying, though, was the recent news informing them that the evacuation was to end that night with the last boat leaving under the cover of darkness during the early hours of the following morning. Laycock, however, was ordered to evacuate himself and his staff so that he could maintain command of his two remaining battalions in North Africa and Cyprus. There was little time left and Laycock handed over command of his remaining force on Crete to George Young and instructed him to negotiate surrender as and when the time arrived.

Suddenly, during the early hours of 1 June, and completely out of the blue, Ogden-Smith received the order to get his men to the evacuation beach as quickly as he could. It was 2.00 a.m. but maybe there was still time. He and his men scrambled and fell down the rugged narrow track. When they reached the bottom of the hill they found the road leading to the harbour was still packed with troops making their way to the evacuation areas. Ogden-Smith made it to the beach. It still looked a desperate situation but somehow he and his men managed to get on the last landing craft to leave the island. He later wrote in his diary:

> *How we got to the beach without breaking my ankles I don't know. Palmer got a box of ammo there although he had 3 broken ribs. After a while we got on the last MLC to leave.*

For George Young and those left behind on the island the situation had become impossible. With the last evacuation vessel having left Crete, Young gave his men the option to try and make an escape by whatever means they could. There were some, albeit in small numbers, who managed to get off the island in small craft and somehow survived the long journey to North Africa. Some even stayed on the island and took to the hills, where they joined forces with Greek and Cretan civilians to form partisan groups and continued to cause the German occupying forces significant problems for years to come. But for most, particularly the wounded, the war was over.

Safely back on board the *Abdiel*, Ogden-Smith noted that the ship was packed but there were very few faces he recognised. With him were Derek Thirkell-White and Peter Wand-Tetley. They had also been fortunate to get away. He wandered around the cramped ship as best he could to see if there was anyone else he recognised. There were very few, though he was pleased to find Jos Nicholls.

Not that Ogden-Smith knew it at the time, but from the 800 commandos of Layforce that had gone ashore just five nights before he was one of only twenty-three officers and 186 other ranks to get off Crete;[7] the other 600 were listed as killed, wounded or missing, although many were taken as prisoners of war. Amongst those taken prisoner were Ken Wylie and George Young, both subsequently to receive the Distinguished Service Order for their gallantry and leadership on Crete.

Safely on his way back to Alexandria, Ogden-Smith could reflect on the past few days. He made himself as comfortable as possible and pulled out his pocket diary, as he had done ever since he had first arrived in Scotland some six months before, and started to record his memories and experiences of the last few hectic days. He wrote more than he had ever written before but then there was so much to tell. He ended his diary entry for Crete:

Back to Abdiel *where they gave us cocoa by the gallon, also gin and lime etc. I could only find a very few of our chaps. Glorious morning. Bathed in Captain's cabin. Felt much less tired. Found out that D Battalion and half of A Battalion left behind in the hills and will not be taken off. White flag at 9 a.m.*

He then listed some of those that had not made it off the island: Ken (Wylie); Doctor; Flood; Savage; Jamie (Kinross); Douglas; Dowling; Lawrence; Maxwell. All were missing. Having brought his diary up to date he went up on deck and looked out to sea. There was a beautiful sunrise and it was going to be a lovely day. At 9.00 a.m. he thought of those left behind as the white flag of surrender cast them into captivity as prisoners of war. He had been lucky. It was a relatively quiet transit back to Alexandria and fortunately there were no air attacks. Utterly exhausted, he disembarked at 5 p.m. and wondered what would happen next. The last six days of his life had been manic. Crete had been a close call.

* * *

The days in the immediate aftermath of Crete were difficult. Not only had Crete been costly for the commandos of Layforce but the British and Commonwealth forces had suffered the loss of nearly 15,000 men, the majority of which had been taken as prisoners of war, although at least 4,000 were listed as killed, wounded or missing; it was also estimated that a further 10,000 Greek troops had been taken as prisoners. The Royal Navy had lost nine warships with a further sixteen ships severely damaged and out of action for many months. Crete had been a brief but devastating campaign and a low point for the Allies in the Middle East, though the battle had also proved to be a costly victory for the Germans, with more than 6,000 casualties, and it would be the only time that such an airborne assault would take place.

The surviving commandos of A and D Battalions were taken to Sidi Bishr to rest and recuperate. They were then merged under a temporary title of Layforce Details and placed under the command of Jos Nicholls, the senior survivor of Crete. Meanwhile, B Battalion had sent a detachment to the port of Tobruk, which was now under siege, and the commandos of C Battalion were recalled from Cyprus to prepare for operations in Syria.

For the survivors of Crete there was uncertainty as to what would happen to them next. With only a handful of officers and little more than a hundred fit men there were insufficient numbers to constitute any kind of force. Besides, they had done their bit for now and there was even talk of them returning to their former units – but Ogden-Smith was clearly hoping for something more interesting. Nonetheless, for the time being at least, it was to be a welcome break. Having completed his report, he enjoyed the days that followed. He was able to spend his time swimming, relaxing and dining. He was also able to write home and inform his family that he was alive and well.

Apart from the question of what to do with the commandos, the excessive losses in the Mediterranean meant that the Royal Navy was no longer in a position to provide ships in support of amphibious operations, and so the decision was made to disband Layforce. Back in London, Churchill was disappointed. He had not been impressed by the higher command's use of the commandos in the Middle East and so ordered the formation of a new organisation called the Middle East Commando: a battalion-sized unit based at Geneifa under the command of Laycock and made up of the survivors of Layforce.

Layforce as an organisation was to formally disband at the end of July. While some of the surviving commandos elected to return to their former regiments, others decided to remain in the Middle East. Ogden-Smith was one of the latter and was keen to remain where he was rather than return to the artillery. Unfortunately, he first found himself in hospital in Alexandria for a week having contracted a fever. At one stage there was even talk of sending him home on one of the convoys, but he was pleased when that idea seemed to disappear. As he recovered in hospital it gave him more time to write home. His letter to his mother was written on an airgraph form and dated 2 July 1941:

I'm so sorry that letters have been infrequent of late but we are only allowed one form each week and there is a shortage, which has meant no writing because it's not worth sending by ordinary post. My last letter from you was dated April 24th and that's very good going! Well I was glad to hear from you and to have your cables. I hope you had mine to say that I arrived back quite safely from Crete. Now I am waiting to hear where they are going to send me next. I'm afraid it will be back to gunnery again but I'm trying for something interesting. I really feel Wendy's husband and your second born ought to have a few more pips scattered around, don't you?

The letter continues about family-related matters and it is clear how strong his relationship with his mother was. Understandably, he avoided making any reference to the hardship of Crete, or the fact that he was in hospital at the time of writing.

Ogden-Smith left hospital to find that A Battalion had broken up. Following a short period of sick leave he went to Cairo to catch up with some old friends and then to the Royal Artillery's base depot where he was delighted to be granted his request to transfer to the Middle East Commando. He even managed to meet up with his older brother, Tony, who had recently arrived in North Africa with the Green Howards. It was now 25 July and there was much to catch up on. The following day Ogden-Smith wrote:

> *Got permission to go to Commando Base Depot at Geneifa. Stopped at Quassâsên and found Tony looking fairly well. Had very good evening and left 26th for Geneifa. Arrived back late. Told to stay on. Posted to Jack Owen. No 2 Troop.*

It would be the last time the two brothers would see each other as Tony would later be captured after heavy fighting at Tobruk during

7. After escaping from Crete, Ogden-Smith briefly met up with his older brother, Tony, in Egypt during July 1941. Tony had recently arrived in the region with the Green Howards and would later be taken as a prisoner of war at Tobruk. (Annie Bland).

1942 and became a prisoner of war. Now back at the familiar setting of the camp at Geneifa, Ogden-Smith was back amongst some friendly faces. Not only was Jack Owen there but so too was Peter Wand-Tetley and Jos Nicholls.[8] It was now a matter of waiting to find out what was to happen next.

At the end of August Ogden-Smith found out that he was to be one of five officers and twenty other ranks sent to a training school at Latrun in Palestine to attend a specialist demolitions and language course. Just as he was about to leave Geneifa he received a rather interesting cable from his wife. The message was brief but in his diary he wrote:

I received a cable from Wendy as I left saying Geoff [Appleyard] wanted me if I could get away. All impossible now but there is a hope of promotion here if only I could make my brain function.

For the time being he had to park any idea of returning home but he must have wondered why Appleyard had been in touch and wanted to get him back. For the time being, at least, he focused on his new course.

Located on a strategic hilltop some fifteen miles to the north-west of Jerusalem, Latrun was a place of historical importance and one of the first things he did was visit the monastery. The course was to last three weeks and it would provide a pleasant change from Egypt. He would also be taught basic Arabic, although he had no natural flair for the language, or any other language for that matter. His diary entry of 11 September suggests he was not overly happy:

Find work very hard as cannot learn Arabic, just cannot remember. Demolitions seem ok. No letters from Wendy or anybody.

Two weeks later he finished the course, in his own words *'fairly satisfactorily'*. Then, just days later, he was summoned to the headquarters in Jerusalem where he was given the news that he was to take over command of the school at Latrun as Major Borrowdale, who was presently in command, was to be transferred elsewhere.

While taking command of a training school might not have been what he was expecting, the thought of promotion to the rank of captain was exciting: it was what he had been after for some time. In a letter home to his mother dated 3 October 1941 he wrote:

I have suddenly shot up in the world and shall be in a day or two a captain and the commandant of a school!!!

Four days later, while returning to Latrun, Ogden-Smith crashed his truck and ended up in hospital for nearly a week with four stitches in his head. While in hospital he found out there was to be an inquiry into the accident, although he was advised that he would probably get off lightly. In the end, Ogden-Smith had to pay for half the damage to the truck. His part of the bill came to a sizeable £6 10s. Although he was informed that he was to be allowed to keep his appointment as commandant of the school, confirmation of his promotion to captain had seemed to stall.

All of a sudden Ogden-Smith seemed less keen on staying in Palestine. Perhaps it was the thought of Appleyard's offer that he had first heard about from Wendy a month before. There may even have been more information about the offer in the two letters he received from his wife while in hospital, although this is unlikely given that it was typically taking two months to receive letters from home and Wendy would have known better than to mention details of operational units or individuals in her letters to her husband. No doubt, though, he would have often thought about Appleyard's offer and he might well have guessed it would have something to do with amphibious operations along the lines they had plotted together in Scotland all those months ago. If so, it would be far more like how he had imagined commando operations to be – unlike how he had fought at Crete. It might have been because the promotion he clearly yearned for had seemingly stalled, for the time being at least, that he was now put off becoming commandant of the school, or there may have been words said outside of the inquiry into his accident. It may have been a combination of all these things, but whatever was going through his mind during his six days in hospital, he knew it was time to leave the Middle East and now was the perfect time. Appleyard's offer was just what he needed to get away. All he needed now was permission to do so.

Within days Ogden-Smith had seemingly got his way, subject to confirmation from the Royal Artillery Depot in Egypt; perhaps the feeling was mutual given all that had gone on in Palestine during the past couple of weeks. Having handed over his responsibilities at Latrun, he reported to the Royal Artillery Depot in Egypt on 26 October. His diary entry for the day was very brief but clearly captures his excitement:

Arrived RA Depot at 1.30. Saw Commandant. UK OK!!

A month later he was in Cairo and waiting for a ship back home. It took some time to get a passage back to England but at the end of November he finally received news that he was to go home. Having made his way to the transit camp at Tewfik, he met up for one last time with Peter Wand-Tetley who had elected to stay in the Middle East. Wand-Tetley would be the only one of Ogden-Smith's close friends from his commando days in the Middle East to survive the war. Having remained in special operations in the region, Wand-Tetley first joined the Long Range Desert Group and was then amongst the first members of the newly formed Special Air Service. He then joined the SOE in 1943 and operated in the Balkans.

As for Ogden-Smith's other close friends, Jos Nicholls had left the Middle East, having volunteered to undertake special operations with the Chinese Army then at war with Japan. The specialist unit, known as Mission 204, was trained to act as guerrillas with the Chinese, and when Japan entered the Second World War, the unit became part of the Chinese 6th Army. Sadly, Jos Nicholls was killed in May 1942 doing what he loved best, operating behind enemy lines in the jungle; he was twenty-five years old. In his last letter to his mother, Nicholls wrote:[9]

> *I am writing this letter in case an emergency should arise, and not in any gloomy spirit, but I don't like leaving things to chance, and to put it bluntly, you will only get this if I am scuffered, and in that event, there are some things I should like to say. I know it's easy for me to say 'don't grieve for me', but I have had a marvellous life in every way, particularly since the war started. I think I have crammed into it more experience and interest than most people can who are ten years older than I am. I know it's not the right thing to say, but I have loved the war; I have had with me for nearly two years of it, the finest lot of chaps a man could wish to command. We've been through quite a lot together, and have a mutual respect and comradeship that nothing in this world can break. Together we fear nothing, in this world or the next. No man could ask for more of life than this.*

Derek Thirkell-White would also lose his life in action. He was killed while serving with No 1 Commando in Greece during November 1943; he was twenty-six years old.

Having said goodbye to Peter Wand-Tetley, Ogden-Smith boarded RMS *Strathaird* the following day for the long transit home. It was the last day of November. It would take two months to get home but life on board the *Strathaird* was reasonable. She was 22,000 tons and had been built as a cruise liner for the Peninsular and Oriental Steam Navigation Company but was now operating as a troop ship. Having picked up some Italian prisoners of war at Port Sudan, the *Strathaird* eventually made it back to England via Aden, Kenya, South Africa, the Caribbean and the United States. It had been a long but trouble-free voyage home.

CHAPTER THREE

The Small Scale Raiding Force

IT WAS A COLD day at the end of January 1942 when Ogden-Smith finally disembarked at Liverpool. He had been away exactly one year. The train journey to London seemed to take forever but he finally arrived at his parents' house in Piccadilly. Wendy was there to meet him and the following day they left for Balcombe and then for a few days together in Bournemouth. His two weeks of leave soon passed and he returned to find the Royal Artillery had approved his transfer to the new unit. On 16 February, Ogden-Smith met up again with March-Phillipps and Appleyard for the first time in more than a year.

The three men talked at length over dinner. March-Phillipps explained that he and Appleyard had further developed their earlier idea of forming a small force to carry out amphibious raids against the enemy. They had been instructed to hand-pick a small group of men for a new unit – to be led by Gus, with Apple as his deputy. The unit had been formed as No 62 Commando so that it would not attract too much attention but it was better known as the Small Scale Raiding Force, or SSRF. It had been formed within the structure of the SOE, although it was placed under the operational control of Combined Operations. They had already been to West Africa with a Brixham trawler they had acquired called the *Maid Honor*. Its non-naval appearance had made it ideal for operations. Posing as a neutral

Swedish yacht and operating from Freetown, they had reconnoitred the coastline as it was believed to be sheltering German submarines that were using the river deltas in Vichy West Africa as refuelling depots for their Atlantic operations. The daring exploits of the small crew included their significant part in Operation Postmaster, one of SOE's classic amphibious actions: seizing a powerful German diesel tug and immobilising a large Italian merchantman in the port of Santa Isabel on the Spanish island of Fernando Po. For their West African adventures, March-Phillipps had been awarded a Distinguished Service Order and Appleyard a bar to the Military Cross he had won earlier for bringing back two SOE agents from France.

Having brought Ogden-Smith up to date with the story so far, March-Phillipps explained that he had now been told to form a larger group, of between fifty and sixty men, to carry out small-scale raids across the Channel. These raids were to be against German strongpoints and signal stations along the northern coastline of France and the Channel Islands with the aim of gathering vital intelligence and capturing German prisoners of war for interrogation. Not only would these raids provide the Allies with vital information, but German troops would have to be diverted to garrison duties along the coast of northern France and in the Channel Islands to prevent further raids.

It had been a marvellous evening catching up with his friends once more and the idea of joining this elite unit excited Ogden-Smith very much. He could not wait to get started. While he was sorting out the paperwork for his transfer to his new unit, March-Phillipps and Appleyard went house-hunting in Dorset. They were essentially looking for a house spacious enough to accommodate up to thirty officers with large grounds suitable for use as a training area, and from where they could gain reasonably easy access to the ports of Portsmouth, Poole and Portland, from where they could mount their amphibious raids.

They soon found a large house located at Winterbourne Kingston about ten miles from Poole and just off the Dorchester–Wimborne

Minster road. Built in 1622 and restored just before the First World War, Anderson Manor, with its beautiful gables and bay windows, and symmetrical in all its detail, was a quite stunning large Elizabethan manor. It was set in the countryside and provided a suitably quiet location with extensive grounds and beautiful gardens. It had been closed up for the war but all it needed was some electricity and running water. For March-Phillipps it was perfect.

Ogden-Smith officially transferred from the army to the SOE on 30 March 1942 and was posted to the SSRF in the temporary rank of captain at STS 62 (Special Training School 62), the SOE's cover name for Anderson Manor. All SOE officers were transferred to their allocated STS on a probationary basis for the first month, after which the arrangement was for the individual to remain at the school subject to a month's notice on either side. He now worked for the SOE and not the army, and everything from pay, training, assignments to promotion would now be the decision of those within the SOE. Every officer was briefed on the Official Secrets Acts of 1911 and 1920 and was then required to sign a card to confirm their understanding. All were liable to be returned to the War Office or dismissal without notice in the event of any breach of confidence, discipline or disclosure by them to any unauthorised person of information which the officer may have acquired in the course of their duty. Also, the disclosure to any person of emoluments received would lead to instant dismissal. The rules were very strict.

On 20 April Ogden-Smith drove down to Dorset to report to Anderson Manor. The final approach to the manor took him along a straight road lined with lime trees and crossing the narrow River Winterbourne. He could not fail to be impressed. It was early April and as he walked through the immaculate grounds of the manor the sea of bluebells, violets and primroses made a most wonderful sight and those dry hot days in Egypt, where he had been exactly a year before, already seemed a distant memory.

He soon realised he was among an elite group of individuals. One of those he was introduced to was twenty-seven-year-old

Graham Hayes, who had been born in the same Yorkshire village as Appleyard and was a boyhood friend of his. Before the war Hayes had served as an apprentice seaman on a Finnish four-mast barque sailing from England to Australia, and later as a craftsman with a furniture-making company in London. The outbreak of war in Europe had brought an end to his furniture-making skills and he wanted to serve in some capacity that gave him freedom, adventure and anything but regular working hours. Hayes had joined the army and became a member of the first parachute battalion. He had been reunited with Appleyard the previous August in time to become part of the five-man crew who sailed to West Africa in the *Maid Honor*, and for his part in the successful operations he had been awarded the Military Cross. Also part of that same *Maid Honor* crew in West Africa was a tall, blond Danish second lieutenant called Anders Lassen. Still only twenty-one years old, Lassen had grown up on a large estate and from an early age had enjoyed freedom that most modern-day parents would never contemplate. He was happiest when in an outdoor environment, where he excelled in field craft and was a crack shot with any kind of weapon. Lassen had the strength of a lion, the charm and good looks that were the envy of many men, and the personality and character that made him a law unto himself. He was also an excellent seaman and had been just the kind of man March-Phillipps had been looking for – in return, the young Dane would demonstrate a loyalty to him that was second to none. The other officers were John Burton, Ian Warren, Lord Francis Howard of Penrith, Tony Hall, Hamish Torrance, Patrick Dudgeon, Peter Kemp, Brian Reynolds, Graham Young and Henk Brinkgreve of the Dutch Army.

The men came from all backgrounds and across a wide range of army units but all had been hand-picked by March-Phillipps. The SSRF would eventually be made up of about half officers and half men of other ranks. These included a Free Frenchman, André Desgranges, a sergeant major called Tom Winter, who had served with Graham Hayes in the parachute battalion and had joined the team at the same time, and a sergeant called Alan Williams. Amongst the other ranks were several German-speaking refugees from other nations, including French, Danes, Dutch, Poles and Czechs. Some were now operating under a British alias name to protect their identity in case of capture. One example was forty-two-year-old Richard Lehniger, a Jewish Sudeten German who was operating under the alias of Richard Leonard. Born in Bohemia, then part of the Austro-Hungarian Empire, Lehniger had served against the British in the First World War, after which he had studied in Prague where he met his future wife, who then held the chair of the Student Social Democratic Party at the university. After the Nazis had overrun the Sudetenland and Czechoslovakia in 1939, he and his wife were considered to be possible political dissidents and so both had made their way to England. In March 1940 Lehniger had enlisted in the Pioneer Corps and served for two years before he joined the SSRF and changed his name to Richard Leonard. Another example was a twenty-six-year-old Pole called Abraham Opoczynski. Born in Lodz of Russian parents, Opoczynski had escaped to England after the German invasion of Poland and had joined the Pioneer Corps in March 1940. Because of his fluency in a number of foreign languages, Opoczynski was enrolled as a member of the SSRF but using his alias of Sergeant Adam Orr of the Queen's Own Royal West Kent Regiment. There was also a Dutchman, Jan Hellings, working as Private Hollings, and so it went on.

Anderson Manor was soon adapted for use by the team, although every effort was made to preserve the heritage of the old building and to prevent any damage. A generator provided the electricity and water was pumped from a well. Some of the rooms were turned into an armoury and an explosives store, while outside in the remote parts of the grounds the men had set up various pieces of equipment to aid their training programme, including an assault course and a pistol-firing range.

It was soon down to intense training, with the aim of turning the men into masters of their new role. A lot of the training was familiar to Ogden-Smith but there were also plenty of new skills to learn, with much of their time spent in boats, learning how to navigate at sea and how to handle the boats in all kinds of weather and conditions, as well as how to land on beaches in small landing craft. Time was also spent in the water getting used to swimming in full clothing and keeping their equipment and weapons dry. March-Phillipps strongly believed that his men should be fully independent and they should not rely on anything or anyone if operating behind enemy lines, and so a lot of time was spent on Exmoor at night and learning how to survive in rugged conditions. Ogden-Smith always enjoyed the hard training and never tired of watching Lord Francis Howard dipping his hand into a mess tin and pulling out greasy pieces of bully beef with his fingers. There were also long marches, usually operating in two-man teams, to see how well the men functioned when living solely on special rations, carrying their 45 lb pack and having to sleep rough. One such walk started and finished in Exeter and took the men 120 miles in four days over rough ground and tracks. There were also challenges, such as being dismissed one day and told to reassemble at a location a hundred miles away the following day – how the men got there was entirely up to them. There was also a trip to the Lake District to undergo further training in hill-walking and rock-climbing, and specialist training in the use of explosives, grenades and other weapons such as pistols and sub-machine guns.

To take a small raiding party across the Channel, March-Phillipps had secured the use of one of the Royal Navy's experimental motor torpedo boats, MTB 344, but colloquially known to the men as the *Little Pisser*. Commanded by Lieutenant Freddie Bourne of the Royal Naval Volunteer Reserve and with a crew of eight, the *Little Pisser* could carry a raiding party of about twelve men, which was ideal given that it was never intended for the raids to be any bigger. It was a brand new boat and was capable of reaching speeds in excess of forty knots. It was also designed to sit low in the water to make visual detection that much harder, although this meant it

8.   MTB 344, known colloquially to the men of the Small Scale Raiding Force as the *Little Pisser*. Commanded by Lieutenant Freddie Bourne and with a crew of eight, the *Little Pisser* could carry a raiding party of twelve men and was capable of reaching a speed in excess of 40 knots.

was limited in speed when operating in rough sea and was not a particularly comfortable ride for the raiders when travelling at high speed. In such conditions the men would get the occasional soaking during high speed transits across the Channel.

The MTB did have one major advantage when operating close to enemy-occupied coasts, as it was able to run relatively silently on an auxiliary engine. This would enable the raiding party to creep as close as they could to the enemy shore without being detected. The *Little Pisser* had also been adapted to suit the team. MTBs were capable of carrying two eighteen-inch torpedo tubes but these had been removed to provide room to carry a light landing craft to get the raiding party from the MTB to the shore. The team had acquired a number of small collapsible flat-bottomed assault boats, made with wooden bottoms and canvas sides, known as Goatleys. Each Goatley weighed just over 300 lbs (150 kg) and was capable of carrying a dozen or more men; these could be assembled quickly in just a few minutes. They also had a Dory, a small, lightweight and shallow-draft boat made of wood with a flat bottom, high sides and a sharp bow. It was just under 20 feet (6 m) in length and could also carry a dozen or so men but was not as flexible as the Goatley once ashore. Finally, the *Little Pisser* had retained two Vickers and two Lewis machine guns to provide some form of defensive armament, although, in reality, these would prove little match for a more heavily armed German E-boat.

The men soon learned how to operate in mist, gales and strong currents, and what to do when a successful landing could not be achieved through an engine breakdown on the boat. Ogden-Smith soon made his mark in this new and elite group of men, so much so that he was considered to be in the top echelon of the officers. His promotion to the rank of captain had now been confirmed and he would soon get his chance to lead a raid. He had also managed to persuade his brother, Bruce, to leave what he considered to be his rather mundane wartime existence as a driver to join the team, and so the SSRF now had two Ogden-Smiths within its ranks: Captain Colin Ogden-Smith and Private Bruce Ogden-Smith.

By the middle of June, training was complete and the SSRF was ready to carry out its first operation. There then followed a period of raids being planned and then having to be cancelled for a variety of reasons, such as fog or unusually bad weather in the Channel or because of the occasional problem with the *Little Pisser*'s engine. It was also at a time when an increasing number of cross-Channel raids were being planned by different units and so clearance to conduct a raid could not always be obtained. There were other considerations to take into account, such as the amount of moonlight on the night – too much moonlight would add a further risk when approaching the enemy coast and once ashore.

The number of planned raids that were cancelled – sometimes when the raiding party had got as far as mid-Channel – had proved a source of frustration for Ogden-Smith over several weeks. Finally, on the night of 14/15 August, the first raid took place.

The operation, called Barricade, was to carry out a reconnaissance to the north-west of Pointe de Saire on the eastern coast of the Cherbourg Peninsula, where a German radar site had been located and was proving to be a continuous nuisance to Allied shipping in the Channel. The raiding party would also carry out an attack on an anti-aircraft-gun site known to be in the area. March-Phillipps was to lead the raid with Appleyard as his deputy. Ogden-Smith was included in the group of eleven selected to take part in the raid, with the others being: Graham Hayes, Anders Lassen, Hamish Torrance, Graham Young, André Desgranges, Alan Williams, Jan Hollings and Tony Hall.

From the briefing at Anderson Manor it was clear that they could expect a difficult landing and approach to the site, along what was a rocky part of the French coastline. Late in the afternoon the raiding party boarded a truck and left the manor for the Royal Naval coastal base of HMS *Hornet* at Gosport, where the *Little Pisser* was waiting. Just before 8.30 p.m. they boarded the MTB and minutes later they set off. Speed was always important. German E-boats were freely operating in the Channel and being fast, well-armed and generally better suited to operating in the open sea, they posed a real threat. Unfortunately for the raiding party, the port engine of the *Little Pisser* had been causing problems for some days before and it was to be no better that evening. The crossing had to be carried out at a reduced speed of 25 knots for the first hour but then the engine cut out altogether, leaving the MTB to proceed towards France on just its starboard engine at a speed of little more than 15 knots. The final part of the crossing had a further risk as they had to navigate along parts of known shipping lanes to avoid the minefields and so they had to take great care to proceed without being spotted or heard. It was nearly midnight by the time the MTB finally arrived off the French coastline. They were now over an hour behind schedule and establishing their exact position off a darkened coastline was not easy, but once satisfied they were approximately in the right place the starboard engine was cut. The MTB then continued slowly and near silently on the auxiliary engine until they were within a mile of the shore. The men lowered the Goatley and headed for the shore.

By the time they arrived on French soil some twenty minutes later it was nearly 2.00 a.m. and there was little time left to carry out the raid. A strong current had meant that they landed about three miles to the north of St Vaast and nearly a mile away from where they should have been. It was completely dark and there was no ambient light whatsoever. It felt good to be on French soil but there was no time to hang around. March-Phillipps led the men off but the fact they could hardly see further than the man in front meant they were unable to move too quickly. The fact they had not landed in the right place also added to the confusion and the darkness made it impossible to determine exactly where they were.

Moving as quickly as they could across what was challenging terrain, the raiding party proceeded towards where the radar site was believed to be. It was not too long before they could see a building in the distance and, believing it to be part of the radar site, they continued forwards. They came across a barbed-wire fence and could now see a sentry not too far away. They were convinced they had found the right place, but they had in fact stumbled across an enemy sentry post: one of a chain of German defence positions along the northern coastline of France. As the raiders tried to move as quickly and quietly as possible into an attacking position, the sentry heard some noise and called for help. With four German sentries now approaching their position, March-Phillipps, with the advantage of surprise, decided to strike first. The silence was suddenly shattered as the raiders opened fire. As more German sentries emerged from the building, the raiding party continued their attack before making their hasty escape back towards the Goatley, leaving what they believed to be at least three German sentries dead and several more wounded.

The raiding party had not suffered any casualties and fortunately they quickly found the Goatley and eventually made their way back to the *Little Pisser*, although the MTB took some finding. With the raiding party safely back on board, they set off as quickly as they could but it was now nearly 4.00 a.m. and daylight was approaching. They were only mid-Channel when daylight broke, but, apart from a brief scare when they believed they had been spotted by an enemy reconnaissance aircraft, they arrived back in harbour at 7.00 a.m.

Back at Anderson Manor there was time to reflect on the raid and Ogden-Smith wrote in his diary:

Went to France with Gus, Apple, Hamish Torrance, Graham Hayes, Graham Young, Desgranges, Andy Lassen, Sgt Williams, Hellings and Tony Hall. Crossed in MTB 344 and landed from a Goatley folding boat. Apple and Gus navigated almost without incident, though took a long time to find the boat again.

Although they had not managed to reach their main objectives, it had been the first raid carried out by the team and, apart from the problem with the port engine, all had gone relatively well up to and including going ashore. They were disappointed at having been heard by the sentry but their tactics during the fire fight had worked well, and they had been able to inflict losses on the enemy without suffering any casualties themselves. Their hasty departure from the beach had also worked well – again without suffering any casualties – and the journey back across the Channel had been uneventful, albeit they had returned much later than had been planned. Furthermore, they had also let the enemy know that a raid had been carried out. From now on, the enemy patrols and defensive positions along that part of the coastline would have to be reinforced. Overall, they felt they had done a reasonable job.

As Ogden-Smith wandered around the grounds the following morning, he realised just how good the manor was for conducting such operations. Not only did it have the space required as a headquarters and as a training environment, the peaceful and relaxing atmosphere of the house and the beautiful grounds proved a delight when returning back from across the Channel.

While the SSRF was planning its next operation, other commando units were taking part in a major Allied raid against the port of Dieppe as part of Operation Jubilee. The main objectives of the raid, which commenced at first light on 19 August, included seizing and holding a major Channel port for a short period of time, to demonstrate that such an objective was possible, and to gather valuable intelligence from any prisoners and documents taken during the raid. Unfortunately, though, the raid proved to be a disaster and in the space of just a few hours the casualties suffered by the Allied forces were extremely high; of the 6,000 troops that had gone ashore, more than 3,600 were killed, wounded or taken as prisoners of war, including 250 commandos.

Military leaders would later justify the Dieppe raid by arguing that the harsh lessons learned saved countless lives in the later Allied landings in North Africa and Sicily, as well as in Normandy two years later, but the combination of Barricade and Jubilee in less than a week meant that German forces were increased along the entire northern coastline of France. For the time being at least, there would be no further raids by the SSRF along that coastline.

With the north coast of France considered too risky, the next raid by the SSRF was to be against the Channel Islands but it would not involve Ogden-Smith. The operation, called Dryad, would provide March-Phillipps with an opportunity to carry out his rather bold idea of capturing an entire lighthouse crew and to take away any classified documents and communications signals that could be found. The lighthouse chosen for the raid was located on a chain of rocks called the Casquets, amongst some of the fastest currents in the English Channel and notoriously hazardous to shipping, situated some eight miles to the north-west of Alderney in the main sea route between Southampton and Guernsey. Since occupying the Channel Islands, the Germans had installed their own men in the lighthouse and were now using it as a naval signal station. Its remoteness made it an ideal target for a raid, the raiding party of twelve being led by March-Phillipps, with Appleyard as his deputy. March-Phillipps was keen to give others the chance to take part in their first raid and so he decided to take Graham Hayes, John Burton, Patrick Dudgeon, Francis Howard, Peter Kemp, Henk Brinkgreve, Ian Warren, Tom Winter, Adam Orr and Brian Reynolds, who was operating under the name of Brian Bingham because he was wanted by the Germans for earlier operations in Europe.

The raiding party set off around 9.00 p.m. on the evening of 2 September and arrived off the Casquets just over two hours later. Landing on the face of the rock immediately under the engine-house tower, the raiding party made their way through some barbed wire before scaling the cliff, some eighty feet high. The raiders then split up and rushed the buildings unchallenged. Complete surprise had been achieved and all resistance was overcome without a shot being fired. Seven German prisoners were taken, along with several documents, signals and code books. The prisoners were marshalled by the German-speaking Orr and taken down the rock where they boarded the Goatley under the direction of Burton and Hayes. The last to leave the rock was Appleyard who had suffered an injury during the descent; it later turned out that he had fractured his tibia. Having rendezvoused back with the MTB, the voyage home was made in a rising sea and the men arrived back at 4.00 a.m., seven hours after they had first set sail.

There was much excitement at Anderson Manor the following morning. With seven prisoners and having landed and then escaped without been detected, the raid was a success. Not only had they captured some personnel, the removal of a number of documents and code books would have caused significant disruption across the Channel as the Germans would be required to issue new documents and codes. Morale at the manor had reached a new high. Although Ogden-Smith had not taken part in the raid, he recorded:

MP [March-Phillipps], A [Appleyard], GH [Graham Hayes], Burton, Dudgeon, Kemp, Howard, Brinkgreve, Warren, Winter, Reynolds, Orr, went to 'Yellow Basket' [Casquets]. Brought back 7 and lots of trophies. Very successful.

In a letter home two days later, Appleyard was clearly excited by the night's work, although he played down his injury:[10]

> *I thought you would be glad to know that we had another successful little party the night before last and that this time we brought back seven prisoners – all without a shot being fired on either side! We had no casualties except for two very minor ones, including my ankle, accidentally done in the landing boat.*

It was later discovered the lighthouse crew had been required to check in with Alderney at regular intervals and it was fortunate for the raiders that the lighthouse crew had transmitted a message just five minutes before the raid had taken place, and so it was some time before the Germans realised what had happened. When Hitler was informed of the raid his first reaction was to order the abandonment of the lighthouse. However, the Kriegsmarine (German Navy) had insisted that the lighthouse was necessary for observation in the Channel as well as for navigation and that it would be better protected in future; as a result, the establishment of the lighthouse was increased to thirty-three men.

Five nights later, on the night of 7/8 September, it was the turn of Ogden-Smith to lead a raid. This time the raid, Operation Branford, was to be a reconnaissance of the barren islet of Burhou, another outpost of the Channel Islands situated three miles to the north-west of Alderney. The reconnaissance was to be carried out with a view to using the island for setting up gun emplacements. March-Phillipps needed an expert opinion and there was no one better suited for such a mission than Ogden-Smith, a former artillery officer. The plan was for March-Phillipps and Appleyard, who was still recovering from his earlier injury, to navigate the MTB to the drop-off point and then for Ogden-Smith to lead the raiding party ashore. Ogden-Smith was naturally delighted to get the chance to lead a raid and there was further good news when he found out that his younger brother, Bruce, was also included in the raiding party.

Soon after 9.00 p.m. the *Little Pisser* set off from Portland and set course for Ortac Rock, three miles to the west of Alderney and midway between Alderney and the Casquets. It was a nice evening and the sea was relatively calm, which meant the MTB made good time – until about an hour into the crossing when the port engine cut out again. Unfortunately, this had now become a familiar problem with the *Little Pisser* and was due to problems with the fuel pressure in the engine. With the continuing threat of German E-boats and with only one engine, the decision was reluctantly made to turn round and head back to Portland.

It was undoubtedly the right decision but Ogden-Smith was disappointed to have the mission aborted. However, as the MTB was heading back towards Portland the mechanic continued to work frantically on the engine and succeeded in getting it started once more. Faced with the decision of resuming with the mission or returning to Portland, March-Phillipps made the decision to turn back towards the Channel Islands and resume the operation. Ogden-Smith was delighted.

It was about 11.00 p.m. when red lights were spotted ahead, indicating the position of Alderney harbour. Speed was reduced but even on a relatively calm night the sea was getting rougher as the MTB closed towards the rock. It was a tricky approach through a maze of dangerous rocks and ledges but a few minutes later Ogden-Smith could see the Casquets off the starboard side and then the unmistakeable shape of Ortac Rock off the port bow. The MTB manoeuvred inside the Burhou reef and the anchor was dropped soon after midnight. Ogden-Smith and Lassen plus six other members of the landing party climbed into the Goatley and paddled the 600 yards to the shore. In his report after the raid, Ogden-Smith noted:[11]

Shore was reached at 0028 hours and the landing made on the reef at a place about 60 yards west of the southernmost point of the island. The rock here is steep and in steps. The boat was held off by kedge anchor. There was no noticeable tidal set and the sea was absolutely calm.

Leaving two to guard the Goatley, including Lassen, Ogden-Smith led the five other raiders – his brother Bruce, Rifleman Roe, Privates Mitchell and Mayer, and Corporal Edgar – across the wet broken rock, covered in slippery seaweed. Ogden-Smith stopped to look ahead. The rock was now steeper and he knew the only building on the island was a house some 400 yards away. When they arrived at the house they found it partly demolished by artillery fire. Ogden-Smith divided the group. Three men, led by Edgar, went to the western area of the island while Ogden-Smith led the other two to cover the central part of the island and the east. There was no sign of any recent habitation and nothing had been done by the Germans to fortify the position.

The reconnaissance required an assessment of the island. The size of the island, its rock structure and drainage all had to be assessed, as did the ease of approach to the island and the ability to move once on it. The island was approximately 700 yards long and 300 yards wide at the eastern and western extremes but only about 150 yards in the central part of the island. The central ridge was bare granite, rising slightly above the ridge line, with soft grass and soil below; the granite had been split up by irregular rain water channels up to one foot deep, with the average slope being between 20 to 30 degrees, making walking across the area difficult and hazardous. There were frequent lengths of smooth granite rocky outcrops throughout the island and the foreshore was made up of broken granite rock with pools and the occasional long narrow gulley. From the island Ogden-Smith could see that the lighthouse on the Casquets was back in action, coming on at 1.00 a.m. and flashing three times every twelve seconds, and that the new crew were using a lamp to signal in Morse code to the German forces on Alderney, possibly because the radio transmitter had not yet been repaired. He also noted that a searchlight came on briefly at Cap de la Hague on the coast of France.

It was soon time to leave. They had been on the island just an hour but everything had gone to plan and so the raiding party made its way back to the Goatley and then returned to the MTB. It was around 4.30 a.m. when they arrived back at Portland, seven and a half hours after they had first set off.

Back at the manor, Ogden-Smith concluded in his report:[12]

Landings in similar weather would seem possible anywhere west of the southern reef and east as far as the gulley immediately below the house. Similar conditions exist on the north shore. The higher the state of the tide the better. Packed artillery or mortars or loads requiring two or three men are practicable. Wheeled or track guns would present great difficulties as there are no sand beaches and all landings would have to be made over rock. There are a number of places where high-angle guns could be placed, though the ground is very soft where the grass grows. There is sufficient crest clearance except immediately behind the rough ridge rocks.

He then brought his diary up to date with a short entry:

Gus and Apple navigated and I took ashore Bruce, Edgar, Roe, Mitchell and Mayer for a Recce. All covered in 1 hour and uneventful trip home.

After Branford, March-Phillipps started planning the next mission but the extraordinary run of apparent immunity, which had characterised their raids so far, was about to come to a tragic end. The next raid, Operation Aquatint, was to return to the northern coastline of France. It had been three weeks since the Dieppe raid and a month since Barricade on the Cherbourg Peninsula, and so March-Phillipps felt that it was now the right time to return. Fortunately for Ogden-Smith he was not to take part in the raid, nor was his brother, because they had been given a few days rest having taken part in Branford just a few nights before.

The aim of Aquatint was to conduct a reconnaissance mission near Saint Honorine-des-Pertes, a small coastal town near Port-en-

Bessin in Normandy, to collect information about the surrounding area and to take at least one guard as a prisoner. The raid was to be led by March-Phillipps, with Appleyard as his deputy, and the rest of the twelve-man team were Graham Hayes, John Burton, Francis Howard, Tony Hall, André Desgranges, Tom Winter, Alan Williams, Jan Hollings, Adam Orr and Richard Leonard. The raid was originally planned for the night of 11/12 September but had to be cancelled when fog made it impossible for the raiding party to locate its landing site.

The following night, 12/13 September, the fog had cleared enough to allow the operation to take place. Having left Portland, it was just after 10.00 p.m. when the MTB arrived off the coast of France. They were close to Barfleur and so the MTB reduced speed to avoid detection and to manoeuvre around the enemy minefield lying off the shore. They finally reached their dropping-off point just after midnight.

The plan was to land to the east of Saint Honorine and then scale the cliffs to take up a position to the rear of the houses along the seafront, from where they would carry out a swift attack and take some prisoners. Although the area was believed to be free of any concrete gun emplacements, it was believed there was a network of coastal batteries capable of providing interlocking arcs of gunfire, with German infantry carrying out foot patrols in the areas.

It was extremely difficult to locate their intended landing site and in the end the landing party opted for an inlet which they believed to be Saint Honorine. It was, in fact, Saint Lauren-sur-Mer, about two miles to the west of their intended landing position. Because he was still recovering from a fractured tibia suffered during the Dryad raid less than two weeks before, Appleyard once again had to remain aboard the MTB while March-Phillipps led the eleven-man raiding party ashore in the Goatley.

It had already passed midnight. Having reached the shore, they found they were too close to houses to leave the Goatley and so they

Like his two brothers, Ogden-Smith was a territorial soldier and served with the
...ourable Artillery Company before the war. He is pictured here at Windmill Hill camp
...ng 1930 and is in the extreme left corner of the picture wearing a jacket, behind and to the
...of the NCO in the front with a pipe. (Angela Weston).

On 17 September 1938, Ogden-Smith married Wendy Moore in St James, London. The
...ding provided a rare opportunity for his family to be pictured together. Colin is second from
...alongside his mother and father, and his younger brother, Bruce, is front right. The oldest of
...hree brothers, Tony, is centre at the rear. (Angela Weston).

3. (*Above, left*) Ogden-Smith pictured just before the war. (Charmian Musgrove).

4. (*Above, right*) One man Ogden-Smith formed an instant friendship with on joining No 7 Commando was Geoffrey Appleyard. The two men first met in Scotland in December 1940 while subalterns under their influential troop commander, Gus March-Phillipps. All three men would again serve together with the Small Scale Raiding Force during 1942. Awarded the Military Cross twice and the Distinguished Service Order, 'Apple' was killed on 13 July 1943 while serving with the Special Air Service during the Allied invasion of Sicily.

5. Home to Ogden-Smith during his time with No 7 Commando and Layforce was the Landing Ship Infantry HMS *Glengyle*. Built for the Glen Line as a fast passenger carrying cargo ship, and capable of 18 knots, the 10,000 tons *Glengyle* had only recently entered service but had immediately been identified as suitable for military service as a large landing ship.

6.   Like Ogden-Smith, Jocelyn Nicholls
lunteered for the commandos from the Royal
Artillery. The two men served together with
force in the Bardia raid and during the heroic
rguard action on Crete. Nicholls led G Troop
in both actions and fought with distinction
on Crete, most notably during the heavy and
lecisive fighting on 28 May 1941 when he led
iis men against German paratroopers holding
a hill top, in what is believed to have been the
first bayonet charge by commandos. Nicholls
/as fortunate to escape from Crete and briefly
ommanded the survivors of Layforce. He later
volunteered for a special unit, Mission 204,
ading Chinese guerrillas against the Japanese
it was killed in Burma on 11 May 1942 while
operating behind enemy lines.

Tony Ogden-Smith served with the Green
vards during the war and was taken prisoner
obruk. He and Colin last saw each other in
pt during July 1941, soon after Tony had
red in the region. (Annie Bland).

8.   After the disbandment of Layforce,
Ogden-Smith remained in the Middle
East to find out where he was destined for
next. He is shown here (centre) relaxing
with colleagues at the end of 1941.
(Charmian Musgrove).

9. In early 1942 Ogden-Smith returned home where he was wante[d] by a small and specialist unit to car[ry] out daring raids across the English Channel. (Charmian Musgrove).

10. Ogden-Smith pictured during 1942 while serving with the Small Scale Raiding Force. (Charmian Musgrove).

11. Wendy Ogden-Smith. After a lengthy period in the Middle East, Ogden-Smith's [ti]me based at Anderson Manor [in] Dorset with the Small Scale [Raid]ling Force gave him valuable [pe]riods of respite at home with [his] wife in between conducting [dar]ing raids across the Channel. Wendy gave birth to the [co]uple's only child, Charmian, in December 1943. (Charmian Musgrove).

12. Bruce Ogden-Smith was persuaded by his brother to take part in special operations and he served with Colin during 1942 with the Small Scale Raiding Force. After the SSRF was disbanded, Bruce served with the Combined Operations Pilotage Parties and was subsequently awarded the Distinguished Conduct Medal and Military Medal for his daring reconnaissance of several beaches along the Normandy coastline during early 1944, prior to the Allied invasion of Europe, including the beach that would later be designated Gold Beach on D-Day. (Angela Weston).

13. Jed training included a course at the Parachute Training School at RAF Ringway, Manchester, during which at least three jumps were made; two from a tethered balloon from height of 700 feet, one by day and one by night, with the third jump being made at night fro an aircraft at low level. (via the Dallow family).

14. The Jedburgh Training School was established at Milton Hall in February 1944. While some of the oak-panelled rooms inside the marvellous building were converted into classroo and lecture halls, the surrounding grounds became assault courses and gunnery ranges. The pistol range pictured here was set up in the walled garden on the south-eastern side of the m house. Ogden-Smith was an instructor at the school but volunteered to lead one of the Jed teams into France because of a shortage of suitably trained officers.

Ogden-Smith pictured at Milton Hall in 1944 prior to departing for France with team ncis. The number one relates to him being the team leader.

16. Arthur Dallow, the young radio operator of Francis, was a far more rugged individual than his appearance might first suggest and was just nineteen years old when he parachuted into France behind enemy lines. Dallow was fortunate to ape with his life at Kerbozec, having hid brambles just yards from where Ogden-mith had been killed while the Germans searched the area. He is pictured here at the end of the war after the award of the Military Medal for gallantry. (Courtesy of the Dallow family).

17.   The farm at Kerbozec with its eleven hectares and streams running through from the nearby mill presented a scene of tranquillity. Home to the Fiche family, the farm was regularly used by the Maquis during the German occupation. (Eliane Lebas).

18.   (*Above, left*) Louis Fiche was the first of the Maquis to meet up with Ogden-Smith at Lopers. Fiche was twenty-three years old and the leader of the section at Querrien. He could speak excellent English and took Ogden-Smith to his farm at Kerbozec prior to Francis being re-united for the first time in four days. (Eliane Lebas).

19.   (*Above, right*) Eliane Fiche was sixteen years old when the men of Francis were in hiding Kerbozec. She was present on the fateful day of 29 July 1944 when she witnessed the atrocities carried out at the farm. (Eliane Lebas).

(*Above, left*) Also staying at Kerbozec during July 1944 was André Burbaud, the cousin of is and Eliane Fiche. After the Allied invasion of Europe, André had been sent to stay with relatives in the quiet countryside of Brittany because his parents believed it would be safer him than at the family home in Paris. (Armelle Burbaud).

(*Above, right*) Pictured at the end of the war, the hide at Kerbozec, marked with an arrow, re Ogden-Smith and his team were in hiding on 29 July 1944. The hide was spotted by a local , a collaborator, while out walking and its position reported to the Germans, which led to the ng battle that followed.

Although of extremely poor quality, this is the last photograph of Ogden-Smith (standing ar on the right) and was taken just days before he was killed. Also standing at the rear are other two members of Francis; Arthur Dallow on the left and Guy Le Borgne in the centre. eling front right is Barthélémy Guyader, the radio assistant who had joined Francis when first parachuted into France. (via Marcel Moysan).

23. Pictured at the end of the war, the pl[...] where Ogden-Smith spent the last mome[...] of his life, marked with an 'x'. He and Maurice Miodon had held the Germans o[...] for long enough to allow the rest of Franc[...] to make their escape. Finally, Ogden-Smit[...] decided to make a break for it but as he tr[...] to leave the ditch to climb over the hedge [...] was hit in the stomach by a burst of mach[...] gun fire and fell back against the base of t[...] tree. Moments later he was dead.

24. Maurice Miodon was twenty-two years old and a sergeant serving with 4 (French) SAS when he joined Francis after becoming separated from his own unit. He died fighting alongside Ogden-Smith at Kerbozec and the two men were later buried side by side at Guiscriff.

25. The elderly farmer, Louis Fiche, was brutally slain for sheltering Francis at Kerbozec. After killing the 71-year-old Fiche in a field, the Germans burnt the farm house as a furth[...] appalling act of reprisal. (Eliane Lebas).

26.   Oberfeldwebel Walter Rubsam served with 609 Feldgendarmerie de Quimperlé and led his unit at Kerbozec on 29 July 1944. After the area had been liberated, Rubsam's name repeatedly emerged in connection with atrocities carried out during the German occupation. As the most senior member of his unit at Kerbozec, Rubsam was ultimately held responsible for the atrocities committed at the farm and after the war he became the subject of an investigation by the British War Crimes Investigation Unit. Rubsam was arrested in April 1946 and he finally admitted to giving the order to burn the farm. However, with no evidence linking him to the allegation of the maltreatment of Ogden-Smith's body after his death, the WCIU closed the case at the end of 1946. (National Archives WO 309/843).

27.   Oberfeldwebel Eugen Schneider of 609 Feldgendarmerie de Quimperlé. As Walter Rubsam's second-in-command at Kerbozec on 29 July 1944, Schneider was the other member of the unit to be specifically accused of war crimes at the farm. Schneider was arrested at his home in Mannheim in April 1946 but, as Rubsam's deputy, he simply denied any responsibility at the farm that day. As with Rubsam, there was no evidence linking Schneider to any maltreatment of Ogden-Smith's body and the case was dropped by the British War Crimes Investigation Unit. (National Archives WO 309/843).

28.   After the war, the Ogden-Smith family agreed to the request from the local French community to have Colin laid to rest in a special vault alongside his two French comrades, Maurice Miodon and Gérard Gaultier de Carville. The reinterment of Colin Ogden-Smith to place at Guiscriff Communal Cemetery on 28 July 1946; the second anniversary of his death. Ogden-Smith is in the centre with De Carville on the right of the picture and Miodon on the left. The service was attended by a figure reported to be in the thousands.

29.   Today the site of the old farm at Kerbozec provides a peaceful scene. The farm house wa rebuilt after the war, although the stone walls of the old outbuildings remained, and is now privately owned.

30. In 1985, Général Guy Le Borgne was honoured to return to Kerbozec to present the elderly Marie-Jeanne Fiche, now ninety-six, with the Legion d'Honneur for her extreme courage during the Second World War, having repeatedly sheltered members of the Maquis at her farm as well as Francis during July 1944. (Eliane Lebas).

For sixty-four years the cross made by Marie-Jeanne Fiche commemorating Ogden-Smith remained at the foot of the tree where he had died but it was felt that it merited a better ce, and so in 2008 it was moved and placed on private land with a ceremony involving the al community. (via Eliane Lebas).

32. The two surviving crosses have now been placed on communal land and can be found together just a few yards from the entrance to Kerbozec. The cross on the right has the plaque with the names of the three to have been killed at the farm on 29 July 1944 – Louis Fiche, Colin Ogden-Smith and Maurice Miodon. The cross on the left is Ogden-Smith's original cross made by Marie-Jeanne Fiche in 1944.

33. Each of the three Ogden-Smith brothers had a daughter. Angela Weston (daughter of Bruce on the left), Annie Bland (daughter of Tony in the centre) and Charmian Musgrove (Colin's daughter) are shown together in 2012 shortly before Charmian's death. (Sam Gardner).

The author pictured at Guiscriff cemetery with three members of the local community, f whom had been teenagers in 1944 and had met Ogden-Smith during his time operating nd enemy lines. On the left is Denise Le Moine whose father had sheltered team Francis s farm at Fornigou. On the right is Louis Kervédou who had been a farm hand at Lopers n Ogden-Smith first made contact with the Maquis. Second from the right is Eliane Lebas, daughter of Louis Fiche, the elderly farmer at Kerbozec, who had been so brutally slain for tering Francis moments after Ogden-Smith had been killed.

The site of the Battle of Kerbozec today, looking down the sloping field from the farm se towards where Ogden-Smith and team Francis had been in hiding. The hide was where trees can be seen today in a projected line just to the right of the tyre hanging from the tree.

36.   The author addressing the local community (in French) in July 2012 at the 68th anniversary of the Battle of Kerbozec.

37.   Seventy years on, the marvellous Eliane Lebas has never forgotten the gallant Major Anglais. Her personal memories of Ogden-Smith and immense help over so many years have been instrumental in enabling this story to be told.

dragged it 200 yards to the east. With Howard left to guard the Goatley, the main party made its way to the east of the houses and inland ready to make their attack. The previous commando raids had meant that the German forces along the northern coast of France were still at a high state of alert and there had also been changes to the German's fortification plans, with many infantry strongpoints now situated along the French coastline.

As March-Phillipps led the men back towards the beach they were spotted by an enemy patrol. Using Verey lights to illuminate the beach, there followed a horrendous battle lasting several minutes. A searchlight on top of the cliff scanned the area as the Germans raked the beach with machine-gun fire and grenades. The raiding party was in a desperate situation but fought back with great courage and all but one succeeded in getting back to the Goatley. They got the Goatley off the beach and had got as far as a hundred yards out to sea when a devastating burst of machine-gun fire destroyed the boat. The raiders were now left to try and swim for the safety of the MTB but a strong tide made this all but impossible and they reluctantly abandoned the idea and made their back to the shore. Four of the raiding party – Francis Howard, Tony Hall, Tom Winter and André Desgranges – were captured immediately and three others were killed. Two of those killed were Alan Williams and the Jewish Sudeten German, Richard Leonard (Lehniger), but the most significant loss of all was the fearless Gus March-Phillipps.

The Verey lights had also illuminated the MTB just 300 yards off shore and it, too, now came under attack. Faced with no alternative, Appleyard took the *Little Pisser* further offshore and cut the engines to make it appear that it had set course for home. Instead he waited for things to quiet down and assessed the damage to the craft. The starboard engine and gearbox had suffered considerable damage but after a short period of relative calm the MTB made its way back towards the shore, where Appleyard and the crew waited for nearly an hour.

9. The Small Scale Raiding Force was formed and led by Major Gus March-Phillipps. Gus was Ogden-Smith's troop leader when No 7 Commando formed. The two men first met in December 1940 and it was during their training in Scotland that the idea of the SSRF was born. Having then gone their separate ways, Gus would track down Ogden-Smith for his new and highly specialised SSRF. To many, Gus was the archetypal English hero but he would be killed while leading a daring raid on the night of 12/13 September 1942.

The silence was suddenly broken by shells bursting overhead. The MTB had been spotted once more and was now under attack from out at sea. Finally, with all hope of picking up the raiding party gone, and with the enemy closing in, Appleyard reluctantly headed back out to sea. The damage to the *Little Pisser* meant the Channel would have to be crossed at a reduced speed and it would be getting light in a few hours, and so he took the MTB straight through the minefield. The gamble worked. As daylight started to break, the MTB was spotted by Allied aircraft and escorted into Portsmouth harbour, where Appleyard stepped ashore. It was nearly 7.00 a.m.

The three members of the SSRF killed on the beach, including Gus March-Phillipps, were buried two days later in the local churchyard at Saint Laurent-sur-Mer. While the Germans believed they had accounted for all of the raiders, four of the men had succeeded in getting away. Three of those – John Burton, Jan Hollings and Adam Orr – had managed to swim further down the coastline and make their escape, although they were all subsequently captured. While Burton would survive as a prisoner of war, the two Europeans – Jan Hollings (the Dutchman, Jan Hellings) and Adam Orr (the Pole, Abraham Opoczynski) – were less fortunate. Both were handed over to the Gestapo for questioning and their fate remains unknown, although Orr is known to have escaped with two others while being moved from a prisoner-of-war camp during the bitterly cold early weeks of 1945, in what later became known as the Long March. What happened to him after that is not known but he is believed to have died on 12 April.

The fourth member of the raid to have made his escape was Graham Hayes. Having swum well away from the carnage he went ashore further west along the coast. The full details of what happened to Hayes over the next six months are not clear but he was smuggled away by the French and apparently made his way to Spain with the intent of returning to England. However, such was the German infiltration of the French Resistance at the time, it appears that Hayes was betrayed and handed over to the Germans. He was then incarcerated in the notorious prison at Fresnes in Paris, where the Germans held captured members of the SOE and the Resistance, and it was there, on 13 July 1943, that the brave Graham Hayes was executed by the Germans.

Operation Aquatint had been a complete disaster. Not only were some of the men killed on the beach, but there had been no suitable back-up plan to help the others. There would have to be changes to the way the team operated if such a tragedy was to be avoided again. While the men of the SSRF were all experienced commandos, and had expected the inevitable losses, none of them had expected losses on such a scale. As Appleyard reported to SOE headquarters in London, those left back at Anderson Manor were given a few days' leave, with Ogden-Smith returning to Balcombe to spend four days with his wife. His diary simply recorded:

Gus, Graham Hayes, Burton, Howard, Desgranges, Hall, Winter, Williams, Orr, Leonard, Hellings all lost east of Cherbourg at St Honorine. Apple did not go ashore. There is now much doubt as to what will happen.

Despite the devastating loss of two of his closest friends, Gus March-Phillipps and Graham Hayes, Appleyard remained undaunted as he was given command of the SSRF on promotion to the rank of major. He knew that life had to go on and the raids should continue: it was what Gus would have wanted and would have expected. Having suffered so many losses on Aquatint, the SSRF received some augmentation from men of No 12 Commando. It was now time for Appleyard to show great strength as the team's leader and for the other officers, Ogden-Smith included, to support him in every possible way so that the team could get back to its winning ways.

It was important to bounce back quickly and, understandably, Appleyard decided to leave the northern coastline of France well alone. The next raid, Operation Basalt, was to be an offensive reconnaissance raid on the small Channel Island of Sark. The raid was to be led by Appleyard. Sark was familiar to him, having been to the island during family holidays before the war. Amongst the twelve selected for the raiding party were Ogden-Smith and his brother Bruce. Also going from the original SSRF team were Patrick Dudgeon, Anders Lassen, Graham Young and Corporal Edgar, with the numbers being made up by Captain Philip Pinckney and other newcomers from No 12 Commando who had just joined the group.

Two attempts to carry out the raid during the third week of September were unsuccessful due to poor weather. The second attempt, in particular, which had taken place on the night of 19/20 September, had proved most frustrating – the MTB had reached as far as Sark, only for the men to have insufficient time to go ashore. While it was a disappointment for all on board, the memories of Aquatint were still fresh in their minds and so there was no point taking unnecessary risks.

The moon conditions now meant the raid had to be postponed for nearly two weeks but finally, on 3 October, approval was given for another attempt to go ahead. As the same men boarded the *Little Pisser* at Portland, the recent losses of Aquatint and the frustrations of the past couple of weeks meant there was a determined mood about the team. It was soon after 7.00 p.m. when the MTB left the harbour.

In addition to the reconnaissance mission on Sark, the raiding party was also instructed to capture some German prisoners and to recover an SOE agent who had been working on the island. The German strength on the island was known to include a heavy machine-gun section, a light mortar group and an anti-tank platoon. Given the disaster just a few weeks before, they could take nothing for granted, but they could never have imagined that the results of the raid they were about to undertake would have repercussions that would stretch far beyond the quiet shores of Sark.

Making their usual final approach on the auxiliary engine, it was around 11.00 p.m. when the MTB dropped anchor. Having successfully gone ashore on Sark, and leaving Young to guard the Goatley, one member of the group went off to find the SOE agent while the main raiding party, with Lassen out ahead in front, clambered up a steep path to the top of the cliff and then along a ridge known as the Hogs Back. In his account after the war, Corporal Redbourn recalls:[13]

When we got to the top of the cliffs, we found barbed wire entanglements. The stillness of the night was only broken by the cry of a seagull or when the wire was snapped with cutters. We fumbled around the whole time in the dark. I was in the centre of the file with Corporal Flint and Anders Lassen, with Captain Pinckney bringing up the rear. When we had gone forward a little we heard a German patrol coming. We all dived off the path and the Germans went past without noticing anything.

After avoiding the German patrol they came across a small group of houses about a mile inland. After watching one large house they were certain there were no enemy to be found and so Appleyard and one of the men went inside. They found an elderly lady who somehow remained completely calm and informed them the Germans were using a local hotel as their headquarters and its annex for accommodation.

The raiding party had already been on the island for two hours and time was short. They made their way quickly to the hotel and arrived to find just one sentry outside. Lassen and Redbourn were given the task of removing the sentry. Redbourn described the moment the sentry was removed:[14]

As there was only one man, Anders [Lassen] said he could manage on his own. We lay down and watched him and calculated how long it took him to go back and forth. We could hear his footsteps when he came near, otherwise everything was still. By now the others had crept up so that all caught a glimpse of the German before Anders crept forward alone. The silence was broken by a muffled scream. We looked at each other and guessed what had happened. Then Anders came back and we could see that everything was alright.

It was around 2.30 a.m. when the raiders stormed into the annex. Inside they came across a hallway with six doors where enemy soldiers would presumably be asleep. Appleyard gave each of his men one room to take with all of his men storming the rooms at the same time. Redbourn later described what happened next:[15]

I rushed into the room allotted to me and heard snoring. I switched on the light and saw a bed with a German asleep. The first thing I did was draw the curtains and tear the bedclothes off him. Half-asleep he pulled them back again. I got the blankets off a second time and when he saw my blackened face he got a shock. I hit him under the chin with a knuckleduster and tied him up. Then I looked around the room for papers or cameras. I got him to his feet still half-senseless and out into the corridor where Captain Pinckney, Andy and the others already stood: there were five prisoners all told. I covered them while the others searched the rooms once more and when this was done we took the prisoners outside.

The raiders quickly led the prisoners from the annex, their hands tied behind their backs. Until that point everything had gone well but one prisoner started shouting – the prisoners were not gagged – and the others tried to make a break. During the commotion that followed, Redbourn recalled:[16]

I had so much trouble with my prisoner. He had got his hands free and we were fighting. He was just on the point of getting away and so I gave him a rugger tackle and we both fell to the ground. He got free again as he was much bigger than me but I grabbed at him and we rolled around in a cabbage patch.

One prisoner had broken free and was shot as he made a break back towards the hotel shouting as he ran. By now Germans were pouring out of the hotel and when the raiders saw how many there were they decided to get away. During the rumpus three other prisoners were shot dead. In his account Redbourn continued the story:[17]

We still had one prisoner who had seen what we had done to the others and so he was stiff with fright and did everything we told him. The most important thing now was to get back to the boat as quickly as possible. The island was waking up and the German headquarters was like a wasps' nest. How we ran. We ran until every step hurt but not in a panic, still in open patrol formation.

The raiding party made it back to the MTB just in time. It was 3.45 a.m. when the *Little Pisser* finally made its hasty getaway, arriving back at Portland nearly three hours later. In the end, the raiders took just the one surviving prisoner back to England. In his report, Appleyard recommended Ogden-Smith for a decoration for his part in Basalt but nothing ever came of it. Ogden-Smith's diary again summarised the raid, emphasising the promotion of his friend Apple:

> _Major Appleyard, [Captain Pinckney – 12 Commando], Dudgeon, Lassen, Young, myself, Bruce, Edgar, [Sgt Thompson, Cpl Flint, Bdr Redbourn, Pte Foster and Greenfield – all 12 Commando] went to Sark. Spent 4 ½ hours ashore after stiff cliff climbs. Found 5 Jerrys, brought 1 back. Had very interesting interview with an inhabitant. All returned safely. Newspapers full of the raid and German threatened reprisals after tying hands!_

In a letter to his younger brother a few days later, Appleyard wrote:[18]

> _Last Saturday night really was fun. We spent over four hours there and had a really good browse round before we rang the bell and announced ourselves. It was so strange to see old familiar places again. Our enforced guest of the evening proved to be a winner! I saw a report yesterday saying that he was considered to be the most useful prisoner obtained by anyone up to date. Yesterday was a very thrilling day – partly spent at the House – in the Prime Minister's private room. He unexpectedly congratulated me. The C.I.G.S.[19] shook hands and said 'it was a very good show!' . . . Wouldn't Gus have been thrilled! That is the type of recognition for which he was always working._

Although the raid had been a typical hit-and-run for the SSRF, it had a much longer and significant effect. In the aftermath of Basalt the Germans issued a communiqué stating that German soldiers had been shot while resisting having their hands tied, thereby contravening international law, and this led to Hitler issuing his Kommandobefehl (Commando Order) just two weeks later. The order stated that all Allied commandos encountered by German forces should be killed immediately, even if in uniform or if attempting to surrender, and made it clear that failure to carry out the order would be considered to be an act of negligence, itself punishable under German military law. In the end, this order would itself be found to be illegal and at the Nuremberg trials after the war German officers who had carried out executions under this order were themselves found guilty of war crimes. Nonetheless, from then on, it changed the way commandos could expect to be treated if captured – not that it seemed to make any difference amongst the men, as they had always known, and accepted, the risks they took.

With the exception of Aquatint, the SSRF was considered a success and the unit was expanded during the final months of 1942. Men were transferred in from other commando units in preparation for an increased number of raids across the Channel. With the SSRF having increased in size, command was given to Lieutenant Colonel Bill Stirling, while Appleyard was finally ordered to go into hospital so that his injury suffered during the Dryad raid a month before could fully recover. Soon after came the announcement of the award of a Distinguished Service Order to Geoffrey Appleyard. It was thoroughly deserved and amongst the many plaudits were letters of congratulations from the Chief of Combined Operations, Lord Louis Mountbatten.

Having safely returned from Sark, Ogden-Smith went home for a couple of days' leave and then travelled up to Birmingham to see some friends. He returned to Anderson Manor a few days later to find that he was soon to lead another raid so that the new additions to the SSRF could experience an operation as soon as possible. With Peter Kemp selected to lead a raid against a signals station on the Brittany coast, called Operation Fahrenheit, Ogden-Smith would lead a follow-up raid on the Cherbourg Peninsula, called Operation Batman, on the first available night after Fahrenheit.

Following another period of waiting for the weather and moon conditions to be just right, the Fahrenheit raid was successfully mounted from Dartmouth on the night of 11/12 November, although no prisoners were captured. There was now a period of just five nights in which the Batman raid could take place. Ogden-Smith's task was to leave Portland and land near Pointe Jardeheu, on the extreme north-west point of the Cherbourg Peninsula, and to gather intelligence and seize any prisoners for questioning. He was to take with him one of the new officers to the unit and a section of six men. Although they were all experienced commandos, none had been on a raid such as this before.

The raid was scheduled for the night of 15/16 November and it was nearly 10 p.m. when the *Little Pisser* set off from Portland. The sea conditions were quite smooth for the time of year and there was only a light breeze. The cloud cover made it a dark night and the crossing took just over two hours. However, the visibility had deteriorated as they approached the peninsula and made it impossible to identify any landmarks. It took until 1.30 a.m. to identify where they were, by which time the breeze had got up and there was now quite a swell, which would have made going ashore in the Goatley extremely hazardous. Furthermore, they were still an hour away from where the drop-off would be made and so the decision was reluctantly made to abandon the mission and return home. They returned to Portland just before 5.30 a.m. after what had been a long and frustrating night.

The weather had now become a limiting factor for the SSRF, particularly the sea conditions, which were now regularly proving too rough for the *Little Pisser*. Although raids were planned, the winter weather was setting in and so ended any chance of further raids across the Channel. During the lull in operational activity, Ogden-Smith took the opportunity to attend a short parachute course at the Parachute Training School at RAF Ringway in Manchester, where he successfully completed five jumps before returning to Anderson Manor.

Elsewhere, higher-level discussions were taking place between the SOE and the Secret Intelligence Service (SIS) as raids being carried out by the SSRF were starting to conflict with other planned operations by different organisations. It was also decided that the raiding experience gained could be put to good use in the North African campaign, specifically where the Allies had recently landed in Morocco and Algeria as part of Operation Torch. In February 1943 a large element of the SSRF – including Bill Stirling, Geoffrey Appleyard, Anders Lassen, Philip Pinckney and Patrick Dudgeon – were transferred to North Africa as No 1 SSRF. They arrived the following month, only to find there was to be no role for the new unit, as the situation in the region had now changed – so it was soon disbanded and the men were instead subsumed into No 2 Special Air Service, under the command of Bill Stirling, with Appleyard appointed as his second-in-command. Lassen, who had been awarded the Military Cross for his cross-Channel exploits, would soon join the fledgling Special Boat Section – later to become the Special Boat Squadron, operating under the Combined Operations Pilotage Parties – as would Ogden-Smith's younger brother, Bruce.

Ogden-Smith was one of a handful retained by the SOE and he remained at Anderson Manor until the SSRF was formally disbanded in April. The unit had existed for just a year but it had produced some of the finest men to have ever served in special operations during the war. Sadly, few would survive. Geoffrey Appleyard was killed just a few months after arriving in North Africa while serving with the Special Air Service. On the night of 12/13 July 1943 he was supervising the dropping of SAS paratroopers in support of the Allied invasion of Sicily when his aircraft went missing. The courageous Geoffrey Appleyard was still only twenty-six years old at the time of his death and in one of those tragic coincidences of war, the date of his death coincided with that of his boyhood friend, Graham Hayes, who was executed by the Nazis on the same day.

Two more former members of the SSRF were to die with No 2 SAS in Italy during the next three months: Philip Pinckney was killed in action on 7 September and Patrick Dudgeon on 3 October. A little over a year before, five brave officers – Gus March-Phillipps,

Geoffrey Appleyard, Graham Hayes, Philip Pinckney and Patrick Dudgeon – had all been part of the SSRF, causing havoc across the English Channel. Now they were all dead. Sadly, but perhaps unsurprisingly given the nature of special operations, they were not to be the last. Anders Lassen had gone on to serve with the SAS and SBS in the Middle East and Mediterranean, rising to the rank of major and being awarded two bars to his Military Cross. After five years of operations, the courageous and seemingly fearless Dane was killed just three weeks before the end of the war while leading a raid at Lake Comacchio in Italy on the night of 8/9 April 1945. Despite being mortally wounded, Lassen continued his attack and enabled his patrol to capture the final defensive position. Through his magnificent leadership and complete disregard for his own safety, Lassen had, in the face of overwhelming superiority, achieved the objectives of the raid, for which he was posthumously awarded the Victoria Cross; he was just twenty-four years old. Anders Lassen remains the only member of the SAS to have been awarded the Victoria Cross, the highest decoration for gallantry.

After the break-up of the SSRF, Ogden-Smith waited to find out what was to happen to him next. There had been various discussions about whether he would be transferred to another commando unit or remain with the SOE. He returned from leave to find out that he was to be transferred to the Air Despatch Section of the SOE. Planning for an Allied invasion of Southern Europe was well underway and the use of aircraft to despatch people and equipment was to prove vital, and so he was to be transferred to an advanced base near Tunis in North Africa, known as Ringlet and part of No 11 Special Operations Depot.

On the evening of 12 August he left England by air courier and arrived at the RAF maintenance airfield at Maison Blanche, just to the east of Algiers, the following afternoon. It was hot and it had been a long flight but there was no one there to meet him. Furthermore, he could not make contact with his headquarters to let them know he had arrived because all the telecommunications were down after a crash-landing by an aircraft earlier that morning, which had taken out all the communications cables. Having hitched a lift into Algiers to report to the Allied Forces Headquarters he tried to telephone Tunis, though it took him two hours to get hold of an officer there. He was told to find some accommodation for the night and to call back the following day. It was not a good start!

The following morning he called Tunis again and was told he would soon receive a movement order and he should get an air passage ticket during the afternoon. Fortunately, everything was soon put in place and the following morning he flew from Algiers to Tunis. It was early afternoon when he landed at the airfield at El Alouina just outside of the city. Having got off the aircraft he found himself, once again, standing around waiting. As he wandered around he could see derelict and abandoned Luftwaffe aircraft, providing a reminder that the war in this part of North Africa had only recently ended. He eventually managed to secure a lift into the city and to the Majestic Hotel. Although it was 1943 the hotel had managed to retain much of its grandeur. It had been commandeered the year before by Rommel's Afrika Korps as a headquarters and the hotel was now being used for the same purpose by the Americans.

Once again, Ogden-Smith was left to try and make contact with Ringlet. Eventually he succeeded and later in the day a captain, who turned out to be the second-in-command at the base, arrived in a car to take him to the camp. It was a rugged journey of about twenty-five miles and lasted over an hour. Fortunately it was late in the day and the sun had gone down; eventually Ogden-Smith arrived at Ringlet, three days after he had left England. He was met on arrival by a major who explained to him that he had been expected but there was no particular job there for him to do. Ogden-Smith was not impressed. He would later be asked to make a report on his time at Ringlet[20] in which his long opening paragraph was solely about his difficulty arriving at his destination, with several expressions of criticism such as: 'there was no representative at Maison Blanche aerodrome' and 'it was impossible to establish communication' and 'after *two hours of telephoning'* and *'where I spent a considerable time trying to contact Ringlet by telephone without success'*. His report then goes on to state:

> *I think I should record here that I had always been told that Ringlet was situated in Bizerta; in fact, it is about 37 km from Tunis and 45 km from Bizerta. On arrival at Ringlet, I was informed by Major Hamilton-Hill that he knew I was coming but that he had no idea with what object. I informed him that my only instructions were that I would find a job waiting for me and that Massingham[21] had made the necessary arrangements. He reaffirmed that he had no job for me to do, but that the first two aircraft to be operated from Ringlet were expected immediately and would be refuelled and despatched that night. At this moment he was told that the Air Liaison Officer, Captain Renton, had collapsed with malaria. I volunteered to take his place and with Squadron Leader Whateley, RAF, proceeded to the aerodrome, where I met Major Wooler who had arrived in one of the aeroplanes. On the following day Major Wooler left for Derna and I continued to carry out the duties of the ALO for the remainder of the moon period.*

It had not been a good start at Ringlet but carrying out the duties of ALO had at least given Ogden-Smith something to do. He started to settle down, although it was still not what he had expected. In a letter to his mother dated 5 September, he wrote:

> *I've all the time in the world though there's nothing entertaining to do, it's just the usual uncomfortably hot and sticky Africa. I quite like the job and hope it will become more interesting later on.*

For the rest of the moon period he worked closely with the RAF's No 328 Wing. The wing had been formed at Proteville, to the north-west of Tunis, for the Allied invasion of southern Italy and during the German withdrawal from Sardinia and Corsica it conducted air attacks against the Luftwaffe's air transport used in the evacuation.

Ogden-Smith was not impressed by the organisation that had gone on before him as he made clear in his report:

I may say that this job was made exceptionally difficult by the complete lack of any previous preparation or liaison with 328 Wing at Proteville. Nevertheless, all serviceable aircraft were flown at the appointed times and a number of successful operations carried out. All operations at that time were refuelling ops, that is the loads were taken on at Derna, flown to Ringlet for refuelling and briefing; the empty aircraft returning to Derna, after refuelling at Proteville, in the morning.

Major Wooler returned to Ringlet in the middle of September and Ogden-Smith was soon considered surplus to the establishment. He briefly worked as the deputy to the commanding officer at Ringlet but the Allies had now secured a foothold in southern Italy and Ogden-Smith found there was neither the work nor the excitement to meet his needs. With the war in North Africa over and the Mediterranean campaign entering its final phase, there was talk of his unit moving out to the Far East but he knew that Wendy was expecting their first child at the end of the year and so a move further east was the last thing he needed. For the first time in the war he felt down and depressed, which did not go unnoticed by his commanding officer.[22] Ogden-Smith was offered an opportunity to volunteer for operations in Greece and Albania but he declined. He needed something operational back home and preferably as soon as possible.

At the beginning of October Ogden-Smith was told that he was to be returned home as soon as possible. He was delighted and the following morning he was up at daybreak and was soon on his way back to Algiers where he was instructed to report to a major who was responsible for arranging his air passage back home. Having arrived in Algiers, the major informed him there would be a flight from Maison Blanche the following day and so he was then driven to a hotel next to the airfield that was being used as transit accommodation for those returning home. It was only sixteen miles to Maison Blanche but he arrived at the hotel to find that conditions were basic to say the least: there was nowhere to sit, nothing to read, no writing materials, nothing to drink or eat, and there were no cigarettes to be found.[23] At least it would only be for one night.

When he reported to the air transport section the following morning he was given the necessary authority for his air passage back home but then, in the evening, he received a note from the major with the bad news that his passage was delayed and that he was to wait at the hotel for further instructions. Having returned to the hotel, he was told that he could not stay there any longer and that he would now have to find his own accommodation until a flight home could be arranged. With nowhere to stay and now out of money, Ogden-Smith telephoned the major who confirmed everything he had been told: there was no air passage back home, for the time being at least, and he would have to find somewhere to stay. For Ogden-Smith, enough was enough. He gave the major his compliments and told him that he would find his own way home!

Just over twenty-four hours later, at 9.30 a.m. on 7 October, a transport courier aircraft of the RAF got airborne from Maison Blanche en route for England. Ogden-Smith looked out of the window as the aircraft climbed out over the coastline of North Africa and took up a heading for Gibraltar. He could see the Mediterranean below and could now relax. At last he was on his way home.

CHAPTER FOUR

The Jedburghs

THE SOE HAD GAINED little support from within Whitehall during its first two years of operations but things had changed in 1942 when its deputy director of operations, Brigadier Colin Gubbins, met with senior British army officers to discuss the SOE's potential role in the liberation of Europe. Amongst the proposals put forward by Gubbins was a concept of a uniformed special forces unit to work with the French Resistance, the *Maquis*. The concept was for a number of small teams of highly trained soldiers, known as Jedburghs,[24] or Jeds for short, to be inserted behind enemy lines to support and co-ordinate *maquis* activities with those of the Allied ground forces following an invasion.

The programme was the brainchild of the SOE, although it was brought to life through the collaborative efforts of the United States' Office of Strategic Services (OSS), which formed a Special Operations (SO) branch in London to shadow the SOE, and the Free French Bureau Central de Renseignements et d'Action. The role of the Jeds would be to act as the broker or diplomat between military operations and the local *maquis* groups after the Allied invasion of mainland Europe had taken place; any suggestion of inserting special forces before the invasion was discounted for fear of compromising the date and location of the main Allied landings.

They would be required to organise, arm and train the *Maquis*, and then co-ordinate various acts of sabotage and guerrilla warfare to assist the advance of the Allied forces on the ground. They would also be required to work closely with other Allied uniformed forces operating behind enemy lines such as the British SAS and the American operational groups.

The Jeds were not to be classed as spies. They were to wear uniform when operating behind enemy lines so that individuals would be covered by the Geneva Convention should they ever be captured and, it was believed, the sight of Allied military uniforms would also boost the morale of the local *maquis* groups with which they would be operating. However, in reality, many German commanders considered the operation of, and acts committed by, partisan groups to be in complete violation of international law and contradicted every principle of clean soldiering in war. The Allies did not share the same view but, despite the best intentions of international law, there was justifiable concern that the Jeds might not be afforded much, if any, protection should they be captured.

The concept of the Jeds was supported in varying degrees by senior Allied commanders but it would require the imagination and commitment of less senior officers, both British and American, to take the idea forward. It would then require the adventure and motivation of the selected volunteers to make it work. This kind of warfare had not been conducted before and so there was no policy laid down or rules by which the game should be played, so much would have to be made up as time went on. The idea was unique in other ways as well, most specifically in the way that the small three-man teams would be made up. No single nation dominated the programme and personnel making up the teams were encouraged to choose themselves. Each team was to consist of a British or American officer, who would lead the operation, with a British or American wireless operator and a French officer in each team responsible for liaising with the local *maquis* groups once on the ground.

It was initially recommended that just seventy teams would be sufficient to undertake the task of liaising with the *Maquis* but this figure was later increased to a hundred teams. It was also recommended that teams should be parachuted well behind enemy lines, at least forty miles, but only into areas where there were *maquis* elements. The idea was approved in October 1943 and the SOE and OSS were given authority to recruit Jedburgh officers and enlisted men as radio operators.

The timing of Ogden-Smith's return from North Africa on 9 October 1943 meant that he immediately came to the attention of Lieutenant Colonel Frank Spooner. Spooner had previously headed up SOE's finishing school at Beaulieu and was now looking to find the right people for the Jeds. Having read Ogden-Smith's file, Spooner decided he was just the type of man he was looking for and so decided to interview him at the earliest opportunity.

The type of officer needed for the Jeds was someone who could lead a small team within the general orders given to him at the start of the mission but was then able to work independently when required to do so. Much of their work behind enemy lines, and the decisions they would have to make, would need to be impulsive. The team leader would have to think on his feet and usually with little time to make a decision. He would be required to create problems amongst the enemy but not in the way he might have been expected to as a soldier, when part of an infantry battalion or within the armoured corps, but more covertly. Furthermore, for the mission to be a success, it would require his team to remain undetected for the duration of their time behind enemy lines.

Spooner was immediately impressed by Ogden-Smith's energy and enthusiasm for an active assignment. Not only did he meet all the personal qualities required of a Jedburgh officer, he had operational experience with the SOE and had operated behind enemy lines. He had also already completed many of the specialist training courses that other volunteers would be required to complete as part of their training. To Spooner, Ogden-Smith was an obvious and natural choice.

While Ogden-Smith was being transferred to the Jedburgh section of the SOE, other British volunteers were being called forward for interview in London while on the other side of the Atlantic similar selection processes were taking place for the American volunteers. Although the recruitment of suitable volunteers was progressing, the numbers being selected were still not enough. The Jedburgh programme would eventually be 15 per cent below its officer establishment. There was a shortage of radio operators too. Specialist training had not produced the numbers required and a shortfall of at least twenty operators now put the whole programme at risk, although a further trawl of Free French forces in Britain and North Africa eventually brought in enough French volunteers.

All Jeds would be required to parachute into France behind enemy lines and so a key part of their training was carried out at the Parachute Training School at Ringway in Manchester, with each man required to complete three jumps to qualify for his parachute wings. From early December the volunteers were sent to the school in groups of fifty, with the men being accommodated at the SOE facility at Altrincham.

It was a cold damp morning in the first week of December when Ogden-Smith arrived for his parachute course. He was amongst the first batch of Jeds to arrive; it would normally be a three-day training course but for him the course would last a week because of the weather and because he would take the opportunity to do two extra jumps. His first jump was from a tethered balloon by day from a height of 700 feet. Although the wind had got up, Ogden-Smith was allowed to jump because he had successfully completed five descents before. Although his exit was considered to be poor his landing was assessed as first class in what was considered to be a strong wind. His second jump was also made from the balloon at the same height but took place at night, and the third jump was made from an aircraft, also at night, from an altitude of just 500 feet. Getting the jump right was obviously important and so Ogden-

Smith took the opportunity to complete a further two jumps at night, including one as part of a night exercise.

Rather than jumping from the side door of an aircraft, such as the Dakota, the Jeds would be required to jump through a hole in the floor of a converted bomber aircraft. Three aircraft types would be used to insert Jed teams into France, two of which were converted British bombers, the Short Stirling and the Handley Page Halifax, operating from Harwell in Oxfordshire and Tempsford in Bedfordshire respectively, and the third was the American Consolidated B-24 Liberator operating from Harrington in Northamptonshire.

The Jeds would also have to jump fully equipped, with each man carrying everything he might need while behind enemy lines. Their standard combat dress was a mix of British- and American-issued clothing. The grey-green camouflaged Denison smock, worn as an outer garment, was British and issued to all airborne units. It was specifically designed to prevent any equipment being caught on the exit hatch when jumping out of an aircraft. The men were also issued with American jump boots and a British helmet. The helmet and smock would be discarded after landing and under the smock was worn normal battle dress. Each man also wore webbing with a pistol holder and various pouches added. There were weapons and ammunition to carry, as well as radio sets, personal rations, first aid kit and various other items required for their mission.

Having completed his parachute training, Ogden-Smith left Manchester with a first-class assessment for all five of his jumps. It would take a few weeks to cycle all the volunteers through Ringway but the reward for passing the parachute course was a seventy-two-hour pass, when most headed for London, after which those who had completed the course early had a short stay at one of SOE's holding schools prior to starting their next phase of operational training.

For Ogden-Smith, the next part of his training took place at Howbury Hall, an eighteenth-century country house near Bedford and home to the Reception Committee School. The school taught SOE agents and the Jeds how to manage drop zones, known as DZs, and how to communicate with aircraft. The techniques ranged from signalling with lamps to more complex methods such as the Eureka/Rebecca system, which had been developed by the Telecommunications Research Establishment at Malvern. The system involved a transmitter fitted in the drop aircraft, called Rebecca, which was tuned to a piece of equipment on the ground, called Eureka, typically marking the location of a DZ. This enabled an aircraft to be guided to within a reasonable distance of a DZ from where the crew could then pick up visual signals from the ground in order to make a drop. It was a very good system, particularly for the crew of the aircraft, although the Eureka equipment was heavy for the agent or operator on the ground and was difficult to conceal. Training was also given using the S-Phone, a short-wave radio telephone that had been developed by the Radio Communications Division at the SOE's research and development station, known as Station IX, at The Frythe, a country mansion near Welwyn in rural Hertfordshire. The S-Phone enabled the drop aircraft to talk to the operator on the ground as it homed in on the ground station, and was a piece of equipment that had significantly improved the efficiency of air drops.

With an excellent assessment for the record, Ogden-Smith completed his course just two days before Christmas and returned home to Balcombe on leave to see Wendy who had just given birth to their daughter, Charmian, the day before. Christmas 1943 proved to be a most wonderful time together, the best ever, and there was much to look forward to in the future. There was also time to reflect on the past year and to wonder how his two brothers were keeping. Tony was now spending his second Christmas as a prisoner of war, although he was safe and well, and Bruce had now returned from the Middle East but was unable to come home for the festive period.

The reason why Bruce had been unable to get home during the Christmas and New Year period was because he was on operations.

He was now a sergeant and serving with the Combined Operations Pilotage Parties, a unit which had been formed in the aftermath of the disastrous Dieppe raid in 1942 and tasked to carry out reconnaissance of potential landing beaches along the northern coastline of France for the forthcoming Allied invasion of Europe. It was essential for the Allied planners to understand the depths of the water approaching possible landing sites, the composition of the beaches and the location of any underwater banks, as well as, of course, the details of any German defences. This was to be no easy task and the only way to gather the information was to put someone ashore.

So while Ogden-Smith was enjoying New Year's Eve at home, Bruce was boarding a motor gun boat at Gosport with twenty-four-year-old Major Logan Scott-Bowden to conduct Operation KJH. The two men were tasked with carrying out a reconnaissance of the beach at Ver-sur-Mer in Normandy, which had been identified as a potential landing beach. Having safely reached their drop-off point, the two men swam ashore under the noses of the German patrols to take detailed measurements and samples along the beach with metal augers, then storing them in special containers for future analysis. The reconnaissance carried out that night was to be the first of several extraordinary beach reconnaissance missions. Once the Americans heard about what the British had successfully achieved, the two men were asked to carry out similar surveys of more potential landing beaches along the Normandy coast. Three weeks later, Logan Scott-Bowden and Bruce Ogden-Smith boarded an X-Craft midget submarine at Gosport. They were then towed by a navy trawler to within a few miles of the French coast where they would spend the next four days. Each day they surveyed the scene through the periscope and then each night the two men swam ashore to gather samples. They eventually completed a reconnaissance of some thirty beaches. These were extremely tiring and hazardous missions. Parts of the coastline were mined and even the beaches that were not mined were patrolled by sentries. Furthermore, the men spent long periods in the extremely cold water, bringing on cramp and severe exhaustion. For these first beach reconnaissance missions from an X-Craft, Bruce Ogden-Smith was awarded the Military Medal and the Distinguished Conduct Medal, while Logan Scott-Bowden was awarded the Military Cross and the Distinguished Service Order.

By the beginning of February 1944 the Jedburgh programme had as many suitable volunteers as it was ever going to get. The SOE and SO had now been formally integrated into the same Special Forces Headquarters, which would assume operational control of the Jed teams, and the first Jedburgh directive had been issued, stating that the SOE and SO could create and control offensive action behind the enemy lines on and after D-Day where the existing communications and organisation were considered inadequate. Although the date for the Allied invasion of Europe had yet to be set, it was now believed to be just a few months away and so all Jed training was to be complete by the beginning of April.

10. While Ogden-Smith was serving with the Jeds during 1944, his younger brother Bruce was in Italy having twice been decorated for gallantry after several extraordinary beach reconnaissance missions along the Normandy coastline of France. (Angela Weston).

The final phase of training was carried out at the Jedburgh Training School at Milton Hall, a magnificent residence set in grounds of more than 600 acres at Longthorpe on the western side of Peterborough in Cambridgeshire, and the ancestral home for the Fitzwilliam family since the late sixteenth century. Identified by the SOE as a suitable location for Jed training, preparations were made and by the beginning of 1944 Milton Hall was ready for training to commence. As a way of not drawing attention to the school, it had not been given 'STS' status like other SOE establishments but was instead known as Military Establishment 65 to the British and as Area D to the Americans. The charm of the old building remained, with the oak-panelled rooms becoming classrooms and lecture halls. Outside the main house, the lawn on the northern side was covered in tented accommodation, while the surrounding grounds and gardens had become training areas, including assault courses. The outer buildings and stables at the eastern end of the house had also been taken over by the Jeds for offices and accommodation, and the barn had been turned into a classroom. For weapons training, the beautiful walled garden to the south-east of the house had become a pistol range and even part of the private golf course had been prepared as a demolition range.

It was at Milton Hall on a bitterly cold day in early February that all the officers and radio operators from the three participating nations were brought together for the first time. Because of his vast experience, particularly in demolitions and weapons, Ogden-Smith had been selected to be one of the school's twenty-six instructors. The first six weeks was full of basic instruction in the vital combat skills and there was plenty of physical training to get everyone up to peak levels of fitness. The basic skills taught covered a wide range of disciplines: map reading and navigation techniques (particularly at night), driving and motor cycle skills, and first aid. Just about all Jed tasks would involve handling explosives, such as plastic explosive, which was waterproof and malleable enough to be moulded into any form but was stable enough to take some considerable abuse

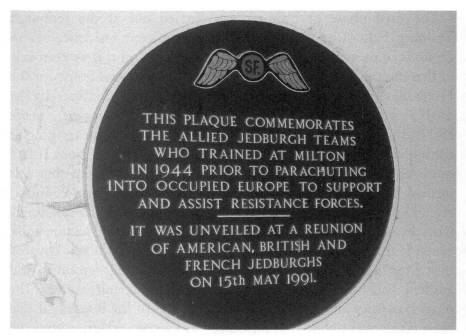

11. A plaque at Milton Hall commemorating the Jedburghs. It can be found in the old stable block, marking the area where the Jedburgh Training School was set up in February 1944.

without exploding. The men were also taught how to lay anti-tank mines and to carry out demolition duties, such as how to lay charges by using a small amount of plastic explosive made up into a series of linked charges to destroy railway lines. This was something the Jeds were taught to do particularly well, not only as a small team but also because of the training that they would give *maquis* groups once behind enemy lines. They were also taught how to fight in a confined area, such as street fighting and when operating in close quarters, including hand-to-hand combat.

As well as being taught offensive tactics and techniques, the Jeds were also taught more covert operations such as how to conduct surveillance and gather intelligence. This involved observation and memory testing, and how to follow someone at night or, equally, note when they were being followed. The men were given lessons on speaking French and lectures on the *Maquis*, including the tactics that they used. There were lectures given by external speakers on the geography, history and culture of France, and the Jeds were even taught how to behave like the French should they ever need to 'become one', including advice on how to dress like a Frenchman and eat like one: simple things like how to hold a knife and fork and when to pour milk into tea did not come naturally to an American. There were also lectures on the enemy, such as how to recognise different types of German vehicles, uniforms and ranks, and they were also told about the type of tactics used by enemy forces on the ground.

There was further training on identifying suitable drop zones and how to organise a 'reception committee'. Identifying and establishing DZs was never going to be easy given that the parts of France where the Jed teams were to operate were mainly made up of small farms with small fields, and there were very few areas of open and uncultivated land. The type of location preferred as a DZ was a pastoral stretch of countryside with no obstacles in the field or wires above, and a clear line of approach for the aircraft with any local features that might stand out at night – such as rivers or lakes, or a church in a nearby village – to aid navigation for the crew. They were also warned about the German radio locator trucks and the sophisticated static listening posts that had been set up in France.

The Jeds were also briefed on the different types of *maquis* groups they would come into contact with. The *Maquis* had proved to be a constant nuisance for Hitler, like a bad rash that had spread throughout France. However, there would always remain divisions between the groups, brought about because of different loyalties within the groups and the politics of France, with the various groups ranging from those that believed in the views of the far right to those of the far left; even religion played a part. There were individual groups operating under the Forces Françaises de l'Interieur, the FFI, while others were French communists and part of the Francs-Tireurs Partisans, the FTP, which had developed after Germany's invasion of the Soviet Union. All these groups could arguably be grouped into two distinct sub-groups: those that were mainly political in their thinking but offered some interest in resistance operations and those that were primarily focused on resistance operations but had some political interest. In reality, there was probably a third group made up of the groups that existed purely to oppose German occupation and had no political interest whatsoever.

The SOE had concerns about the lack of co-ordination between the groups and their operations and there was also an apparent lack of a post-invasion strategy. A power struggle had already emerged, with Charles de Gaulle at its centre, insisting that it should be the Gouvernement Provisoire de la République Française, the Provisional Government of the French Republic, with himself at its head that should decide the destiny of post-war France. There could, therefore, be distinct differences between the strategies of the groups leading to a growing mistrust between them as some leaders appeared to be keener to establish a local power base that could be exploited post-liberation. There was a further problem too, and one that was not insignificant to the Jeds. By 1944 the Germans had managed to step up their campaign against the *Maquis* through infiltration of the groups or by capturing known *maquisards* and turning them into informers by making threats against members of their family.

It was against this background that the Jeds would be inserted into France. It was important for the Jeds to understand the *Maquis* if their missions were to stand any chance of success but it was not for them, or the SOE, to get involved in the politics of France or the differences within the various groups. Indeed, the SOE needed to distance itself from these issues if it was to be as effective as possible. While the British and American Jeds would find it relatively easy to divorce themselves from any internal French wrangling, it was not always as easy for the French member of the team. Each Jed team could expect to work with several hundred *maquisards* within their area, which would be spread across many smaller groups, and so all they could do was to make sure the groups were suitably armed and organised, and trained as best as possible. There was also the hope that once the Allied invasion was underway then the differences between the various groups would recede and all would unite together in the common aim of evicting the Germans from France.

There was so much to learn at Milton Hall, and with three nations working together there were also different pieces of equipment for the men to become familiar with. This was, in the main, a mix of British and American kit, such as British radios and American weapons. The Jed's main weapon was the semi-automatic M1 Carbine with its folding metal stock. Although its 0.3-inch round did not provide the stopping power of other heavier weapons, it was light and easy to use, and for the Jed it proved ideal. Most Jeds also opted to carry the Colt M1911. This 0.45-inch calibre semi-automatic pistol was the American Army's standard sidearm for many years. It was a popular weapon because of its firepower but its main drawback was its limited magazine capacity of just seven rounds. The alternative was the Browning GP35 but it did not have the stopping power of the Colt, although its smaller and lighter 9-mm rounds gave the pistol thirteen rounds and its ammunition was generally easier to come by when in the field. Some Jeds also opted for the British Sten sub-machine gun as a back up to their Carbine. The Sten was a great piece of engineering as far as a weapon was concerned: it was capable of firing its thirty-two rounds in a single three-second burst, although it was only accurate at short range and required strength to maintain any accuracy but it proved easy to operate and robust in the field. It was also particularly popular amongst partisan groups in occupied Europe. It was all a matter of personal choice and the Jeds were also given training on a range of British, French and German weapons.

The men were now being grouped into three-man teams, with the instructors mixing the teams up from time to time so that the men could work with different people and determine, in their own minds at least, who they could get on with and who they could not. During the last two weeks of March, the men were then asked to form their own three-man teams. Because of the shortfall of officers, the instructors were given the opportunity to volunteer to lead a team into France. Although he could have elected to remain behind, Ogden-Smith was amongst the first to volunteer, along with two of his friends – John Marchant, an intelligence officer, and Bernard Knox, an American but a naturalised Briton and a graduate of Cambridge who was fluent in French. Although they did not know it at the time, the three would be amongst the early teams to be inserted behind enemy lines and would lead their teams in the same part of France and at the same time.

It was initially necessary for two officers to team up together and so each British and American officer was instructed to find a French colleague. The French had all adopted a pseudonym, or *nom de guerre,* in case they were ever killed, captured or identified while operating with the Jeds, and their change of name would hopefully protect their true identity and therefore spare their families in France from any reprisals. Some already knew each other while others naturally gravitated towards one another, and with the number of French officers being fewer than had initially been planned, competition was fierce.

One young Frenchman who had impressed Ogden-Smith was Guy Le Borgne. Born in Rennes, Le Borgne was twenty-four years old. He had graduated from the French Army's Saint-Cyr Academy in 1940 as part of a Franco-British friendship initiative and after the fall of France he had escaped to North Africa before making his way to England where he joined the Free French Forces. Like so many of his French colleagues, Le Borgne had waited patiently for the opportunity to return to France and had volunteered for the Jeds as soon as he heard the SOE was looking for volunteers.

Now he was a lieutenant and he would finally get the opportunity he had waited so long for. After four years he could not wait to step back on French soil to play his part in the liberation of his country and, having been born in Brittany, he would be an obvious choice to be dropped in that part of France where his local knowledge would be invaluable. Le Borgne and Ogden-Smith got on very well and during their occasional time off Ogden-Smith would take Le Borgne with him to London to meet his family.

It was then a matter of finding a radio operator for the team and one young sergeant who had caught their attention was Arthur Dallow, a tall and rather thin-looking man with curly hair and thick glasses. Dallow's youthful looks and appearance were deceiving to the casual observer but not to Ogden-Smith and Le Borgne. Dallow was a tough young man. Born in Blackheath on the western edge of Birmingham and brought up just a few miles away in Quinton, he was the youngest of three sons and was seemingly the most troublesome; he even referred to himself as the black sheep of the family. He had left school at the age of fourteen and had since held a variety of jobs, none of which had particularly pleased his parents, who had paid for his education and expected it to have lasted much longer. With an appetite for adventure, Dallow had become increasingly frustrated following the outbreak of war and could not wait to be old enough to join up. In 1942, as soon as he was eighteen years old, he gave up his job as a wood machinist and enlisted into the Royal Armoured Corps. The opportunity to volunteer for the Jeds was just what he was after. Now at the age of just nineteen he was one of the youngest to have been selected for the Jeds.

And so Colin Ogden-Smith, Guy Le Borgne and Arthur Dallow became Jedburgh team number forty-five. The final few weeks at Milton Hall were all about operational training together, both as a three-man team and with other teams because the concept was to drop a number of teams within the same region to maximise their effect across a wide area. This phase included three large exercises, each lasting several days, to bring together all they had learned.

The first, Exercise Spill Out, lasted six days and took place at the end of March – it simulated the kind of conditions out in the field that the teams could expect when operating behind enemy lines. The second, Exercise Sally, was designed to test the command and control aspects of the mission and to test the communications network between the teams and the headquarters back in London. The third, Exercise Spur, took place at the end of April and was designed to test the co-operation and co-ordination aspects of working with partisan groups. This final exercise saw the Jed teams leading the partisans in a mission to kidnap a high-ranking German officer.

By now the Jedburghs had been declared operational but the date for the Allied invasion of Europe was not yet known and so the decision was made to deploy fifteen teams to North Africa at the beginning of May to work with the Allied Forces Headquarters in Algeria. The decision not to insert at least some of the teams into northern France ahead of the Allied invasion would later come under some criticism, although the importance of not compromising the date and location of the Allied landing was, with hindsight, fully justified. However, many Jed teams would end up being inserted much later than perhaps should have been the case.

The decision of when and where to insert the teams – ninety-three teams in all – would have been made at higher levels but the seemingly continuous changes in the command structure at that time could not have helped. The SOE headquarters at Baker Street had now been absorbed by the Special Forces Headquarters at nearby Montagu Mansions, which, in turn, was subordinate to General Eisenhower's Supreme Headquarters Allied Expeditionary Force.

With many of the Jeds heading for North Africa, those left behind at Milton Hall spent the following days going through time and time again everything they had learned so far. There was also time for some sport and other recreational activities and many ventured into Peterborough to the many pubs and hotels, or to go to the dances held at the town hall. At the weekends there was the opportunity to venture further into London to enjoy the many attractions and a wartime social scene that was second to none.

Ogden-Smith was one of those that remained at Milton Hall. He and his team were destined for operations in northern France but they did not know where or when. On 12 May came the announcement that he was promoted to the rank of major and from now on, when on operations, he would operate under the codename of Dorset. Le Borgne, who had adopted the *nom de guerre* of Guy Le Zachmeur, took the codename of Durance and Dallow was to be known as Groat.

Rumours that the Allied invasion of Europe was now not very far away had started to circulate and these had been strengthened by the sight of many heavy vehicles and heavy equipment moving southwards over the past weeks. However, there was to be enough time for one final exercise, Exercise Lash, which was to take place in Charnwood Forest in Leicestershire. It was the last day of May when the teams were transported from Milton Hall and for the next week the forest was to become their home. Ogden-Smith knew this was to be the last chance his team would have to put into practice everything they had been taught during the past five months. The exercise scenario would draw together everything taught so far and would see his team having to organise and control a simulated partisan group using a mix of overt and covert operations. They would need to use the cover of darkness to move around as stealthily as possible and to then strike as and when required at any hour of the day.

It was on the third day of the exercise, 2 June, when two of the teams were ordered to return to Milton Hall. They were told to pack their equipment for another exercise but this time the teams felt that it might be for real. Then, on the morning of 4 June, the two teams boarded a truck for London. The Allied invasion of Europe was now just forty-eight hours away.

CHAPTER FIVE

Team Francis

WHEN THE ALLIED INVASION of Europe took place
on 6 June 1944 the landings took place along a front
stretching sixty miles along the Normandy coast, with
the British divisions going ashore on the eastern beaches and the
Americans to the west.

Normandy had been the preferred landing area for a number of
reasons but the cultural region of Brittany, occupying the north-west
peninsula of continental Europe, was also of strategic importance
because of its deep water ports. With five *départements* – Côtes-
du-Nord (now the Côtes d'Armour) in the north, Finistère in the
west, Morbihan in the south, Loire-Atlantique in the south-east
and Ille-et-Vilaine in the north-east – Brittany has a long, and at
times complicated, history. In the immediate years leading up to
the Second World War, there were some Breton nationalists, who,
although spilt into different factions, were insensitive and hostile to
French democratic ideals and even sympathetic to pro-Nazi feelings.
The most organised and openly separatist movement was the Breton
National Party but, because of its links with Nazi Germany, the BNP
was banned at the outbreak of war, although it was rapidly constituted
following the fall of France and soon became the most active political
party in Brittany under German occupation. Key members of the BNP
began to collaborate with the Germans to some degree, with a view of

securing an independent Brittany, and a number of nationalists even joined the German militia, and over the next few years this led to the assassination of several Breton nationalists by the *Maquis*.

Because of the strategic importance of the region, there were significant German forces based in Brittany, including three paratrooper and two mobile divisions, all of which were available to reinforce Normandy rapidly if and when required. The first Allied special forces inserted into Brittany followed immediately after the Allied landings: these were an advanced party of No 4 (French) SAS, with the aim of establishing two bases – 'Samwest' in the Forêt de Duault and a larger base, 'Dingson', further south. From these bases the SAS, together with *maquis* groups in the area, could hamper and disrupt as much as possible any German attempt to reinforce the area.

The first two Jedburgh missions, named Hugh and Harry, were inserted behind enemy lines in western France during the early hours of 6 June. All the Jedburgh teams dispatched from London were given male first names and the plan was for Hugh and Harry to initially work together and liaise with the *Maquis* in the region before then splitting up to separate parts of the region, with Hugh working in the area between Poitiers and Châteauroux, and Harry working in the western part of the Indre. There were also SAS teams dropped in the area to establish bases from where they could operate and cause as much chaos and destruction as possible.

The first Jedburgh team to operate in Brittany, Frederick, was inserted in the Cotes-du-Nord *département* with one of the main elements of No 4 (French) SAS on the night of 9 June to operate with the Samwest party. Led by Major Adrian Wise, Frederick had been accompanied by team George, led by a Frenchman, Captain Philippe Ragueneau, which had been inserted into southern Brittany to operate with the Dingson party.

By the beginning of July 1944 the Allies had secured the Normandy beachhead: nearly one million troops and tons of equipment had gone ashore. The concern now was the number of German reinforcements rushing to the invasion area. Allied planners believed that the Germans were capable of reinforcing the Normandy region with thirty or more divisions, one-third of which would be Panzer divisions. Special Forces Headquarters in London now decided it was time to step up its effort and informed the Jed teams in France to expect more arms drops and the insertion of more teams.

It was now only a matter of time before it was Ogden-Smith's turn and, at the end of the first week of July, he was informed it was time for his team to go into action. He spent his last hours at Milton Hall writing to his wife. He had not seen Wendy for some time and, as he explained in his letter, the hectic build up and preparations meant that he had not been able to write to her for several weeks; it was also the first opportunity he had to inform her of his promotion to the rank of major. As expected in any letter from a man to his wife informing her that he was leaving the next day for a mission, the letter was personal but he was full of enthusiasm and he was convinced that the mission would make a significant contribution to the time of peace to which he and his wife had both looked forward to so much.

With the letter sent, Ogden-Smith and his team soon found themselves in the back of a truck and heading for London, where they were to be briefed. There was no ceremony as such, as by now many teams had followed the same procedure. The men simply went on their way and during the next two hours on the bumpy route to London they would have to get whatever rest they could.

Having arrived in London, the Jeds were taken to an attractive house in Devonshire Close, just to the south of Regent's Park – one of many small properties used by SOE agents about to go out into the field. It was only a short distance from the SOE headquarters in Baker Street, where they were to be briefed with three other Jed teams.

Over the next twenty-four hours Ogden-Smith and his team were briefed on all aspects of their mission; the only break was for dinner at a restaurant in the evening, followed by a visit to one of the local clubs in the area. The briefing was understandably thorough. Their mission was to organise *maquis* groups in southeast Finistère and their briefing included details of the groups they were to link up with as well as details of the German forces known to be operating in their area. Brittany remained vitally important to the Germans, particularly because of the strategically important U-boat bases along the Atlantic coastline, and so there were some 50,000 German troops known to be operating in the area. These ranged from first-rate divisions to lower-rate units made up of captured Russian soldiers now fighting for the Germans. There was also up-to-date information on known Abwehr (German military intelligence) and Gestapo (short for Geheime Staatspolizei – secret state police) activity in the region, which also included an update on activity involving the Milice (the French collaborative police – effectively a French Gestapo – that had been set up by the Vichy French to assist the Abwehr and Gestapo in their campaign against the French Resistance). The team were also issued with maps and briefed on the terrain and topography of the region. There followed briefings and questions on the communications procedures to be adopted, during which Dallow in particular was quizzed at great length. The men were then briefed on the known friendly agents operating in the region and their pseudonyms, which they were all required to remember – nothing was allowed to be written down.

Ogden-Smith's team was to be called Francis and the overall plan was for his team to be flown across to Brittany with another team called Gilbert. Gilbert was led by thirty-two-year-old Captain Christopher Blathwayt (codenamed Surrey) and consisted of a Frenchman, Paul Carron de la Carrière (whose *nom de guerre* was Charron and codename was Ardèche), and a British radio operator, Sergeant Norman Wood (codename Doubloon). The two teams were to be dropped at different DZs in western Brittany, with Gilbert operating to the north-west of Francis. Francis was to operate in the south-eastern corner of the Finistère *département*, in the extreme west of Brittany and at the westernmost point of continental France. The name Finistère is derived from the Latin *Finis Terrae*, meaning the end of the earth, and with some 800 miles of coastline is considered to be the most coastal *département* in France. Two other teams, Hilary and Horace, were to be dropped further north a week later on a DZ identified by Giles, which would already have been inserted into Brittany the night before Francis and Gilbert, and were to then operate independently in the northern part of the *département*.

It was a plan that would require great co-ordination between the teams once on the ground. The area allocated to Francis had been split into two different zones. One was designated 'A', where there were relatively few Germans with a few *maquisards* who were organised but unarmed. The Germans were known to have a garrison varying in strength from a hundred to maybe double that at Carhaix, and there was another garrison of 180 men at Scaer but the strongest German garrison was at Le Faouët, which was considered to be the centre of an anti-terrorist organisation for south-east Finistère, with between 200 and 500 men. The second zone, designated 'B', was closer to the Atlantic and did not have any *maquis* groups, although it did have a number of well-organised cadres operating in small numbers of two or three, living out in the country or at home. The German garrisons in the Rosporden–Bannalec–Quimperlé area amounted to some 300 men with all the villages south of the Rosporden–Lorient road believed to have fairly strong garrisons composed mostly of Russian soldiers fighting for the Germans.

So much information had been thrown at the Jeds in a short period of time – the remainder of their duration at Devonshire Close was spent examining the maps in as much detail as possible and discussing the mission, while testing each other on the codes and procedures to be used.

The insertion of Francis and Gilbert would bring the number of Jed teams in Brittany to six. Frederick and George had already been in France for the past month and were still operating with the SAS in northern and southern Brittany respectively. Felix and Giles, which were in the process of being inserted just twenty-four hours ahead of Francis and Gilbert, were to operate in the northern and western part of Brittany. Felix was led by a Frenchman, Jean-Paul Souquet, whose *nom de guerre* was Jean Kernevel but operated under the codename Carnavon. Both the other team members were British. One was Ogden-Smith's friend, John Marchant (codename Somerset), and the other was Sergeant Peter Colvin (Middlesex). The team was to operate along the northern coastline with the task of organising and equipping the local *maquis* group as well as reconnoitring and selecting a suitable landing site along the coast where stores could be landed in the future. Giles was a truly tri-national team and comprised of Ogden-Smith's American colleague, Bernard Knox (Kentucky), a Frenchman, Paul Grall (who called himself Lebel and had the codename Loire) and a British radio operator, Sergeant Gordon Tack (Tickie). Giles was to operate to the north-west of Francis and was tasked with identifying DZs for further drops of teams and equipment.

Ogden-Smith's plan was relatively simple in principle, but he knew it would be much harder in practice. For Zone A he intended to visit each *maquis* group, check its organisation and see what weapons and ammunition it had. For Zone B he felt it was more important to view the area and work with the chiefs of each small *maquis* group to make an arms dump. In both zones his team would need to work closely with leaders to get them organised and working together, and they would need training on the new weapons that would be dropped by air during the weeks ahead.

It was the early evening of 9 July when Ogden-Smith, Le Borgne and Dallow, together with team Gilbert, climbed aboard the truck for the final part of their journey to RAF Harrington, where they were to board their aircraft for the flight to France. Also travelling with the Jeds was a member of the SOE headquarters who was there to make sure they were met and briefed at Harrington and he would also assist the men with their specialist clothing and equipment prior to boarding the aircraft.

It was a cool and breezy Sunday evening and there was already some cloud building. A low-pressure system off the east coast of Scotland had produced a north-westerly flow and an occluded front was due to pass through the Harrington area during the early hours of the following morning, bringing the possibility of thunderstorms. There would be no time to hang around at the airfield and any delay could easily result in a postponement of their drop by at least twenty-four hours.

The tiny village of Harrington is situated in a quiet part of Northamptonshire to the west of Kettering and to the south-east of Market Harborough. The airfield to the south of the village had originally been intended for use by Bomber Command but delays in its completion had meant the airfield was instead allocated to the United States Army Air Force as Station 179. Harrington had only been opened just a few months before and was home to the 801st Bombardment Group, known as the Carpetbaggers. The specialist unit flew its missions at night, usually during the moon period, which included dropping SOE agents behind enemy lines and delivering supplies to Resistance groups operating in enemy-occupied countries.

The aircraft used by the Carpetbaggers were modified B-24D Liberators. They were significantly different from their original design as a bomber, and every effort was made to avoid the aircraft being detected at night. The underside of the fuselage and wings were painted non-reflective black to help avoid detection by enemy searchlights, and flame dampeners had been installed on the engine turbo superchargers. Each aircraft was fitted with special radio navigation equipment to help it home in to drop zones and any combat with enemy aircraft was avoided unless absolutely necessary for fear of compromising the mission. With the exception of the top and tail turrets, all the aircraft's armament had been removed; the nose-, belly- and waist-gun turrets had all gone and, because of operating at night, flash suppressors had been fitted to those guns that had been retained. The bomb bay had been modified to carry special supply canisters that would be dropped during the mission. Inside the aircraft all unnecessary equipment had been removed and blackout curtains had been installed where any light might escape, such as covering the waist-gun windows in the fuselage. The lights inside the aircraft were painted red to avoid spoiling night vision and the only other light on board was a small green light that gave off just enough of a glow for the navigator to read his maps and charts. A wooden trapdoor had been fitted over the hole in the fuselage where the belly turret had originally been fitted. The hole proved ideal for dropping parachutists one at a time and was known to the crew as the 'Joe hole'; all the agents were simply known as Joe. The aircraft's crew had been reduced from the standard crew of ten to eight and the crews were chosen for special operations because of their skills in flying at low level at night and because of their pin-point accuracy when it came to navigation.

While Ogden-Smith and his team were making their way to Harrington, the aircrew were well into planning the drop. By now, the Americans were familiar with the routine. The planning cycle started the previous day when the intelligence officer at Harrington was given the list of requested drops for the following night, which were then plotted on to a large map. The following morning, the meteorological officer advised the squadron commander of the weather conditions in the drop areas, after which the squadron commander selected the actual drops for that night; his decision was based on the priority of each request, the type of drop, any likely enemy opposition in the drop area and the availability of his own aircraft and crews. The intelligence officer would then contact the SOE headquarters in London and the drops were agreed for that night.

Each crew then started its planning, with the navigator receiving his list of drops for that night around midday while the intelligence officer gathered as much information as possible regarding known enemy activity and defences en route, *maquis* groups in the area and the type of reception committee that might be expected. Later in the afternoon, the final briefing was held for all the crews involved that night, which included an update on the weather situation for the transit and in the drop area, followed by a final briefing from the intelligence officer. There was then a brief from the group navigator. The routes were planned, as much as possible, to avoid known enemy anti-aircraft defences and used navigation features such as large rivers and lakes, which could be seen by the crew at night. The altitude during the transit rarely exceeded 7,000 feet and as the aircraft approached the enemy coast the pilot would normally descend below 2,000 feet to make the aircraft more difficult to detect by radar; he would then commence the final run-in to the DZ at low level. The pilots had even been taught to fly varying patterns and procedures to disguise the actual point of insertion and, even after making the drop, the pilots would, if possible, continue the deception plan by flying further into enemy territory. Everything possible was done to prevent the Germans from detecting the drop zone.

While the crew were planning and being briefed, the containers and packages required for the night's drops were being prepared and loaded into the Liberator that would take them across the Channel. There was so much to load. The man-sized tubular-shaped containers were full of weapons and ammunition destined for the groups. These containers had a parachute at one end and were fitted with a static line that was fastened inside the aircraft so that when the container left the aircraft the static line would pull out the parachute. Once on the ground the containers were designed to be opened quickly by opening three quick-release fasteners. The total number of containers to be dropped that night was thirty-six, including twelve for Francis that would be dropped ahead of the Jeds. It took two men to load the containers into the bomb bay of the aircraft and packages were loaded through the waist-gunner hatch, where the gun had been removed.

Finally, Ogden-Smith and his team arrived at Harrington, where they were met by the armaments officer who had the responsibility of meeting and looking after all SOE agents prior to them boarding their aircraft. Meanwhile, 300 miles away in the *département* of Finistère, *maquis* leaders of Quimperlé were huddled around their wireless sets listening to the evening BBC broadcast.

The town of Quimperlé, situated in the south-east of Finistère to the east of the market town of Quimper and at the confluence of the rivers Isole and Ellé, was significant to both sides in the region. For the French it was the location of its regional headquarters of the *Maquis*, under the leadership of Capitaine Sylvain Loyer and his deputy, Lieutenant Pierre Brunerie; their task was to direct and co-ordinate the groups operating in the area. For the Germans the town was home to 609 Feldgendarmerie de Quimperlé, a specialist German unit trained in searching for and combating Allied special forces and *maquis* groups operating in the region.

As *maquis* leaders around Quimperlé listened attentively to the BBC broadcast, as message after message was read out, the message they had been waiting for suddenly came across the air waves – 'Yvonne a la gueule de bois', translated as 'Yvonne has a hangover'. A drop was due that night and it would take place in the grounds of Le Moulin de Boblaye, a former mill in a remote location to the south of Meslan, but with less than three hours to go there was little time to make sure that everything would be ready to receive Francis.

Back at Harrington, Ogden-Smith made a final check of his equipment. First he checked his weapons and then strapped his carbine across his chest and inserted his pistol into the holster. He then filled the pouches of his webbing belt with ammunition. Next was a bag filled with extra clips of ammunition, emergency rations and equipment: an escape kit, a first-aid kit including two morphine syrettes in the event of being wounded, a small box of tablets containing Benzedrine to keep him awake and other, more sinister, tablets that were designed to knock others out. There was also the L-pill ('L' for lethal), a glass capsule covered in rubber and containing cyanide for those who opted to take it with them; if necessary, this could be concealed in the mouth and would cause death within minutes if the capsule was crushed and the cyanide swallowed.

Underneath his main equipment, Ogden-Smith fastened a money belt containing 100,000 francs and fifty dollars, which he could use for the requisition of supplies or to pay bribes. The 'Jedset' radio was packed in bags attached to his legs by a pair of straps, with quick-release buckles so that he could free the pack as soon as his parachute had deployed. The package would then dangle twenty feet below him and would hit the ground first in order to reduce his weight on landing and to give him a second's warning that he was about to hit the ground. His pockets were crammed with code books and radio crystals and he also carried a rucksack containing rations and some spare items of clothing; he even found space in his kit to take his Warrior poacher's fishing rod: it was ideal for small packs as it could be broken down into small sections just in case he could find any time to do some fishing! Lastly, he strapped on his parachute. He could barely walk.

By now the Carpetbaggers had inserted a number of Jed teams into France and this was their second Jed drop in consecutive nights. Even at this stage it was possible the mission might not go ahead, as many insertions and drops were cancelled, sometimes even after the aircraft was airborne. The late cancellation of a mission could be for a number of reasons: changes to the weather in the drop area, a sudden change in enemy air activity across the Channel or because a message had been received from the *Maquis* warning that German activity in the area of the DZ had increased. While cancellations were always a disappointment, the operations staffs at both Harrington and at the SOE headquarters in London were keen to ensure there was as little risk as possible up to the point of insertion.

As it was the middle of summer, take-off was to be late that night. The conditions required for a drop to be made were a suitably high cloud base, with only slight layers of cloud to allow sufficient moonlight for the Jeds to be able to see enough of the ground and its detail for the jump, as well as enough light to allow *maquis* groups on the ground to recover the men and equipment. It was coming towards the end of a moon phase but the amount of moonlight was expected to be satisfactory, provided there was not total cloud cover in the area of the drop.

Everything was fine so far and it was now time for Ogden-Smith and his team to board the aircraft. Wearing a parachute and fully loaded with equipment, it was not easy to make the short distance from the hut to the aircraft. Only the outline of the aircraft was visible in the darkness of the night, and it presented an eerie sight.

The Jeds were required to sit on the fuselage floor. There were sleeping bags to help keep the men warm and to make them more comfortable, and they were all given a flask of coffee and some sandwiches. It was cramped inside but as each man tried to get as comfortable as he could, he had time to gather his own very private thoughts. There would have been a feeling of excitement – after all, this was what they had trained so hard for during the past six months – but there would also have been apprehension. There was no way of knowing how the next few hours would turn out, let alone what was in store over the coming weeks or even months. But there would also have been some very personal thoughts and each man would reflect one last time before the aircraft engines kicked into life. Ogden-Smith would, no doubt, have been thinking of his wife, Wendy, and his daughter, Charmian – now six months old, although he had not been able to see much of her – as well as the rest of his family. He must have wondered when he would be back on British soil again or if he would ever return at all.

Finally they were off. It was soon after 10.30 p.m. when the Liberator accelerated down the runway, bouncing a couple of times before climbing away slowly into the darkness. Few local villagers would have seen it, although some would have heard it. They were now getting used to hearing the sound of a lone bomber climbing into the air late at night. At that time of the year it was usually about the same time of the night and it was almost twenty-four hours to the minute since the last aircraft had disappeared into the darkness before heading south; that was team Giles but no one on the ground would have known. It would be nearly dawn by the time the aircraft returned.

Flying at a speed of around 200 mph the transit took two and a half hours before the aircraft was in the vicinity of the first drop zone. It was a long time to sit there with nothing to do. Although there was the opportunity to catch up on some sleep, the reality for most was that their time was spent listening to the drone of the engines and experiencing the unsavoury smell of the inside of a fuselage. There was also time to think. Each man would be rehearsing in his own mind the early part of his mission to the last detail. He would want to make sure the jump went right, as well as wondering what might be waiting in store for them over the coming hours and days.

For Dallow, at just nineteen years old, the reality of the situation he was now in hit him hard. Understandably, he felt the fear but there was no turning back and he would certainly not let anyone down. For Ogden-Smith, this was quite different to what he had experienced before in North Africa, Crete and when crossing the Channel with the SSRF. Although he had been part of a small force before, with only three of them in Francis, he knew they would not have the safety of numbers if they got into trouble, but he had every confidence in his team – neither Le Borgne nor Dallow would shrink when it came to a challenge, and he knew that neither man would let the team down. At last the crew signalled to the Jeds to let them know they had arrived in the drop area.

By now the *Maquis* had been well trained in the selection and operation of DZs, and the reception committee now awaited their new arrivals. It was the responsibility of the groups to recover all, or at least as much as possible, of the equipment dropped but much of the *département* of Finistère was now so heavily garrisoned that such drops were considered quite risky – particularly as the reception committees could be more than a hundred men and women, with all kinds of transportation possible, including horses and carts, to move the equipment.

It was around 1.00 a.m. when the Liberator made its final run-in towards the first DZ. Gilbert was to be dropped first and the men were soon out in the cold air and descending into the unknown. Gilbert would remain the closest team to Francis and was dropped on open ground near the village of Coray, just a few miles from the small town of Scaer and to the east of Quimper. The DZ had been identified earlier in the day by Giles but Gilbert's drop was poor. The Liberator had been forced to fly lower than had been planned because of the cloud and its speed at the point of insertion was higher than would normally be expected, which meant the Jeds had ended up jumping at a lower altitude and higher speed. Although no one was injured during the landing, much of the team's equipment had been damaged or destroyed.

For Francis things were to be no better. The large reception committee was in place to the south-east from where Gilbert had been inserted and had waited patiently for the past hour, and included some of the most prominent members of the *Maquis* in the area. In addition to Loyer and Brunerie from Quimperlé, there was the wealthy André de Neuville, who had been born locally in the village of Arzano and was happy to offer his large family home and its estate to shelter *maquisards* and any Allied special forces operating in the area. Making up the reception committee were other members of the FFI from Quimperlé and three sections led by Paul Tanguy, Pierre de Lépineau and Alexis Méfort.

The designated DZ was a field about five miles to the south of Le Faouët and near the small community of Meslan, where the *département* of Morbihan meets the *département* of Finistère, and the reception committee could now hear the sound of the aircraft as it approached. They knew the area was full of Germans, which made this particular drop more risky than most. Armed *maquisards* had already taken up positions along the small roads and paths approaching the area of drop while others took their positions in small groups ready to recover the containers. The weather was far from ideal for a drop. A westerly air flow had brought moisture from the Atlantic and had resulted in a build-up of cloud and patchy mist in the area. The drop would need to take place soon.

As the Liberator approached in the distance, three bonfires in the shape of a large triangle were lit to mark the drop zone. The bonfires were not small and flames were soon leaping several feet into the air, not only making them visible to the aircraft but also to any Germans in the area. It was a risky business. The aircraft shape could now be seen against the moonlight and a *maquisard* aimed his flashlight towards the aircraft, flashing the nominated letter in Morse to confirm to the pilot that the DZ was in friendly hands. It was now approaching 2.00 a.m.

On board the Liberator, the American crew could see the DZ through the mist. Their first task was to drop the twelve containers and so all the Jeds could do was to sit and wait. Having dropped the containers the aircraft lumbered its way round in a circle before lining up, once again, on the DZ. It was now time for the Jeds, but these were anxious moments for everyone. The longer the aircraft stayed in the area the greater the chance of it being spotted or heard and it would not take long for enemy troops to arrive in the area.

The young American dispatcher removed the wooden trapdoor and stood near the Joe hole. He beckoned the Jeds forward. The usual order for jumping was for the team leader to jump first but Ogden-Smith had agreed to Le Borgne's request to let him jump first as he had always wanted to be the first of the team to land on French soil, and so Ogden-Smith would jump last after Dallow. It was now a matter of waiting until the pilot could see the DZ. The aircraft was now flying lower and lower. Through the Joe hole the Jeds could see the ground rushing past: the patchwork of fields and woods, with the occasional village, were clearly visible but because the ground features were illuminated only by the moonlight, combined with the patches of mist, it was just a murky grey countryside below.

As Le Borgne sat astride the Joe hole, Ogden-Smith looked at his watch. It was now 2.10 a.m. and they had already been in the vicinity of the drop zone for several minutes. He was well aware the Germans might now have been alerted to the DZ and he also knew there was little margin for error when jumping from a large aircraft at low level at night. It would take some time for all three men to vacate the aircraft through the same exit hole, and each had to make sure he vacated the aircraft as quickly as possible to avoid the team becoming too separated on the ground; every second they took getting out of the aircraft meant nearly a hundred yards of separation on the ground. He also knew that any slight navigational error during the run-in, or any error in the aircraft's speed or height, or a delay in vacating the aircraft, could make all the difference between coming down in the nice pastoral field considered ideal for the drop or coming down in dense woodland instead. Not only were there thoughts of being separated on the ground, but the biggest fear for these men, apart from the obvious parachute failure, was coming down into a wall of machine-gun fire, as they hung helpless in their chute or being captured by the Gestapo on the ground.

Any such thoughts were quickly put to one side as the dispatcher shouted that they were running in. Le Borgne checked his static line for the last time, which only a few minutes before he had connected to an anchoring point on the floor next to the Joe hole. Staring down through the hole in the fuselage, Le Borgne could see how quickly the countryside changed in just a matter of seconds: one moment a field, the next a wood. The change in sound as the pilot reduced power on all four engines meant they were now getting closer. The speed reduced further still as the pilot lowered the flaps to the mid-position, allowing him to bring the Liberator's speed down to around 130 mph, just above the speed at which the aircraft would stall. Heartbeats now increased, including that of Ogden-Smith, as this, from the aircrew's perspective, was the part of their mission when the Liberator was at its most vulnerable; being at slow speed and low altitude meant the aircraft was susceptible to any ground fire if it had been seen.

The dispatcher now raised his right hand above his head. A red light illuminated dimly above the men in the fuselage and Le Borgne now dangled his legs through the Joe hole in readiness to jump. He felt the slipstream of the aircraft. He looked behind him to see that Dallow and Ogden-Smith had now taken up their positions ready to follow him out of the aircraft as quickly as possible. It was now too late to think about whether it had been a good idea to have volunteered for this.

Not that Ogden-Smith knew it at the time, but it would be four days before they would all be together again. The aircraft should have been at a height of 600 feet but even to him the height looked lower. The dim red light now turned to green as the dispatcher shouted, 'One-two-three jump!' There was no time to think, just jump. Le Borgne jumped, closely followed by Dallow and then finally Ogden-Smith.

Only those who have jumped know how it feels during those first few moments after leaving the relative safety of the aircraft. The instant sensation of falling was immediately followed by the rush of wind against Ogden-Smith's face and the sudden jolt confirmed that his parachute had opened. He looked up to check that his canopy had fully deployed. It had. Now his feeling of euphoria was followed by the sensations of rapidly descending earthwards in the cold night air.

Jumping out of an aircraft from a height of 600 feet or less means there is barely time for the parachute to open, and very little time is actually spent under the canopy, but Ogden-Smith quickly realised that it was not a pastoral field that awaited him, but trees. Just seconds later he landed with a crunch, the lines and canopy of his chute tangling around him. He had missed the DZ.

Having been the last to leave the aircraft, it meant that Ogden-Smith had overshot the DZ and had come down in dense wood instead. Quickly gathering in his parachute, he immediately realised that he was alone and unable to contact his reception committee. It appeared that he was well and truly separated from the rest of his team. Being behind enemy lines and unsure of exactly where he was, and not knowing what Germans were in the vicinity, he dare not make any noise. It was not a good start!

The darkness and disorientation of being in a dense forest at night meant it would take him some time to work out where he had come down. What was certain, though, was there was no one else to be seen. He moved quietly away. All he could do now was to wait until daylight before he could even start to assess his position and then decide what to do next.

Ogden-Smith had come down in dense woodland in the grounds of Le Moulin de Boblaye, a former mill to the south of Meslan and a few hundred yards from the DZ. The River Ellé, which flows south-westwards from the town of Rostrenen in the *département* of Côtes d'Armor to the Atlantic Ocean, through Morbihan and Finistère, becomes a maze of small tributaries to the south of Meslan. He was now on the wrong side of one of the tributaries and would have to cross the river, although things could have been far worse as he had so nearly come down in the lake at the entrance to the old mill.

The woodland that he had landed in covered over a hundred acres. Furthermore, the terrain was wild and inhospitable, with the fast-flowing river running through a deep gorge with massive rocks; even to the locals the area was known as 'les roches du diable', the Devil's rocks. Fortunately, there were some narrow paths, which meant he could make reasonable time under the cover of darkness and the dense woodland helped conceal his movement. Unfortunately, though, daylight brought thick fog, which did nothing to help him work out exactly where he was.

Before leaving England the team had agreed two rendezvous points. The closest RV was a cave at Rosgrand Wood, which the team would initially make for on landing. However, if things did not go according to plan, or if the team became separated on the ground, then their fall-back RV was a deserted chapel at the village of Saint Fiacre, just to the north of the DZ.

The problem with the fall-back RV at Saint Fiacre was its location just to the south of the small town of Le Faouët, where a German garrison was known to exist. Ogden-Smith knew there was no chance of him making the first RV but before he could think about how to make his way to the fall-back RV he had to first establish where he was. He would then have to decide whether to make for Saint Fiacre or to try and make contact with the *Maquis* in the area in some other way. For now, all he could do was wait. He would have to wait until the fog had cleared before he could determine his position but even then he would probably have to wait until nightfall before he could move on once more.

Meanwhile, Le Borgne and Dallow had been more fortunate. They had also come down in woodland but were now safely in the hands of the *Maquis*. The containers had come down within the area of the DZ and were now being gathered by members of the reception committee. It was now a month after the Allied invasion had taken place and there was optimism and excitement. While Tanguy's section gathered the containers and transported them away from the DZ, Le Borgne and Dallow were quickly led away by one of de Lépineau's men, Barthélémy Guyader.

Guyader was a trained radio operator and had previously worked in England as an aircraft engineer, and so he spoke good English and was considered ideal to stay with the team. Guyader led the team to Rosgrand Wood, situated just to the south-east of Quimperlé. With Ogden-Smith temporarily unaccounted for, Le Borgne, as the deputy team leader, quickly set up his command post in a cave in the grounds of the chateau belonging to André de Neuville. During the afternoon he made contact with two lieutenants, both deputy commanders of their sections, and instructed them to try and locate, or at least establish contact with, Ogden-Smith. Le Borgne then set about organising a reception committee for a drop of more arms and ammunition for the *Maquis*. This was known as a *parachutage* and the first was planned to take place within the next few nights.

The following morning Dallow contacted London and the other Jed teams operating in the area. Communication was through a secure cipher system known as the one-time pad. The pad of sheets, with each sheet being different from the rest, provided a key for enciphering and deciphering messages but obviously required the receiver to have an identical pad. Each sheet was used only once and then destroyed. Messages would always be kept as brief as possible and so the radio operators used a recognised list of abbreviations in their messages. As an additional security measure, Dallow and the other radio operators memorised a number of security checks – such as code words, letters or numbers – which would indicate if the radio operator had been captured and was now transmitting under threat.

Contact with the *Maquis* was to be kept to a minimum and only through a trusted network, and radio contact was made with London or the other teams according to a briefed communications plan. The plan determined the time of day for making contact, according to signal strength and propagation during the day, and the frequency to be used. For Francis, the scheduled times for making contact was between 9.00 and 10.00 a.m. and 3.00 and 3.30 p.m. on the odd-numbered days, and on the even-numbered days the contact times were between 10.00 and 10.30 a.m. and 7.00 and 8.00 p.m. At night transmissions could be made anytime between midnight and 4.00 a.m. The frequency was set by inserting the appropriate crystal and when it was time to transmit, the team leader would inform Dallow of the message to be sent. Dallow would then find an appropriate location, usually up a hill or at least on raised ground, where he would set up his generator, transmitter and sending key, and aerial wire. Although the radio could receive messages with enough power provided by the dry-cell battery, to transmit a message required additional power provided by the generator, which required a second person to hand-crank the generator; this would be done by one of the team or a *maquisard*.

The Germans were capable of jamming the Jeds' radio frequency, as they occasionally did, which meant there were times when the teams could not contact London or even each other. There was also the constant threat of being located through a combination of the German intercept stations, located in the larger towns, and radio detection vehicles fitted with various types of antennae that were operating in the rural parts of Brittany. Once the intercept station had received transmissions coming from a particular area then the detection vehicles would drive around the locality until the exact point of transmission was achieved – this was done by simple triangulation using the bearings of the transmissions received.

The *Maquis* was also in contact with the Jed teams and soon informed Le Borgne and Dallow that their colleagues in Gilbert were unable to make any radio contact with them, or with London, because their radios had been damaged during their drop. Gilbert's priority was to obtain replacement radios and so Dallow was able to relay a message to London on Gilbert's behalf, although back in London the message had been misunderstood and it was temporarily believed back at headquarters that Gilbert and Francis were now together.

Dallow later received a message back ordering the two teams to scatter, but the two teams were not together and had not been since jumping out of the aircraft. Blathwayt had in fact moved Gilbert to the west of Quimper but for much of the next ten days the team could achieve very little as it was out of direct contact with London. Gilbert's radio operator, Norman Wood, would later get his damaged Jedset to work to some degree but he could only get messages relayed to London via Dallow or through Giles, and it would be a further two weeks before Gilbert received a replacement radio.

While all this was happening, Ogden-Smith was still alone, but the fog had now cleared enough for him to make his next move. Avoiding the many tracks and farms in the local area, he made his way towards the chapel at Saint Fiacre. He had to cross fields and pass through woods, and then cross smaller streams before he crossed the main River Ellé. He knew he had to keep well to the south of

Le Faouët because of the German anti-terrorist unit. Having finally reached the chapel, he waited for a while but it was soon obvious to him that no one was going to show up. He knew he could not hang around for long and so he headed off, away from the direction of the town and back towards the area where he had been dropped.

Ogden-Smith was now spending his second night alone but he was confident that Le Borgne and Dallow would have made contact with the *Maquis* and that every effort would be made to find him. Having arrived back at the river he heard the sound of voices in the distance. He could make out that the voices belonged to men having a conversation but, to him, it did not sound like French. What he was hearing, in fact, were men speaking in Breton, a relatively hard-sounding dialect, which, to an Englishman from a distance, was not unlike German. Ogden-Smith could not hear them clearly enough or understand what they were saying. He knew there were Germans in the area and had to decide whether to make himself heard or not. He decided that he could not afford to take the chance.

Not knowing where to go next, Ogden-Smith made his way westwards towards Lanvénégen where he knew a *maquis* group were based. Having crossed the river, he made his way through dense areas of woodland, staying to the south of the town, before finding a suitable resting place in a line of trees on the edge of a field looking down towards the farm at Lopers.

For the next day Ogden-Smith took refuge in an oak tree on the edge of the field. Despite all his wandering around during the past couple of days he was now only a couple of miles from where he had originally been inserted. He knew he had to make contact with someone soon. Then, early on the morning of 12 July, more than forty-eight hours after he had been dropped into France, he spotted a farmer making his way up the field. From his vantage point in the tree he watched the farmer for several minutes. He had stopped about a hundred yards away and was seemingly tending to the potatoes in the field. He looked quite old and was clearly alone. Ogden-Smith decided that it was now time for him to make his

12. From his hide amongst the trees, Ogden-Smith could see down to the farm at Lopers. It was 5.00 a.m. on the morning of 12 July 1944 when he first observed the farmer, Jaouen, tending to his crop just a hundred yards from his hide. After more than forty-eight hours alone since parachuting behind enemy lines, he decided to take a chance and approach the farmer. He was lucky, Jaouen could be trusted and Ogden-Smith spent the next two days at the farm.

move. He dropped from the tree and made his way out into the open field – it was a chance he simply had to take.

It was only just 5.00 a.m. and the old farmer, Jaouen, was surprised to see someone approaching him from the line of trees so early in the morning. He could see the man was quite large and carrying equipment. He could also see that he was carrying a weapon but he was clearly not German and he did not offer the appearance of a *maquisard*. Jaouen did not move and waited until Ogden-Smith got closer. Now he realised the man approaching him was British. Ogden-Smith was lucky: Jaouen could be trusted.

Despite his education and the fact that he had been to France many times before the war, Ogden-Smith's grasp of the French language was only basic and he was far from fluent. When he had first joined the SOE back in 1942 his ability to speak, read and write French had been assessed by the linguists as 'C-C-C', meaning he was only considered to have a working knowledge of the language. Nonetheless, Ogden-Smith could make himself understood enough and so Jaouen took him the short distance down the slope to his farm where he then instructed his son to go to the nearby farm at Kernune, just a matter of 400 yards or so away, to tell the owner, René Le Duigou, there was a visitor at his house.

Le Duigou was already up when he was given the news. He knew the *Maquis* had been looking for the English major and was delighted that he seemed to have been found. He went quickly to Jaouen to confirm the visitor was who he had claimed to be. Ogden-Smith was now in safe hands and it would not be long before he could be reunited with the rest of his team but, having first been given something to eat, he spent the rest of the day catching up on some much-needed sleep.

The sight of Ogden-Smith at the farmhouse was unforgettable for one young farmhand, Louis Kervédou. At just ten years old, Louis could barely remember life before the war. He and his elder brother had been working at the farm for some time and were both used to seeing the *Maquis* come and go but this was the first time they had seen a British parachutist. Nearly seventy years later the memories of the daunting figure of Ogden-Smith with all his webbing and equipment were still vivid for the elderly Louis Kervédou, who recalls the *Major Anglais* as appearing 'so big' to him. While Ogden-Smith was sleeping upstairs in the house, the former farmhand remembers seeing his parachute boots outside the door. 'They seemed so big,' he recalls, but, he adds, the 'warmth and friendliness of the major left an everlasting impression on me and others at the farm.'

While Ogden-Smith slept, Le Duigou made radio contact with the *Maquis* to let them know the English major had been found alive and well. It was now a matter of waiting to find out when and where he would be reunited with his team. Increased enemy activity in the area had meant that it was unsafe to move for a while and the following day he found out it was to be another twenty-four hours before it was considered safe to move on and to establish a safe RV for Francis to meet up once more.

Le Duigou and Ogden-Smith naturally warmed to each other. While they waited for the right time to move, the two men spent hours at the farm talking about their lives and, of course, the war. Ogden-Smith talked about his wife, Wendy, and his daughter, Charmian, and about his brothers, Tony and Bruce. In return, Ogden-Smith learned that Le Duigou had a son, also called René, and that he was in the *Maquis* but along with two other *maquisards*, François Henriot and François Gallic, he had been captured by the Germans; sadly, all three would later be killed. Ogden-Smith and Le Duigou talked into the early hours. These were important moments when they could both reflect on the war and how it had so dramatically changed their lives. They also learned that they had something in common – fishing – and Ogden-Smith talked about leaving the army after the war and returning one day to France with his wife and daughter so that he could spend some time there fishing in the local rivers.

While Le Duigou and Ogden-Smith were waiting to hear more about the next move, two more Jed teams, Gavin and Guy, had been inserted into Brittany. These two teams were to operate some way to the north-east of where Francis was located and would operate in the *département* of Ille-et-Vilaine where there was little in the way of resistance activity, with Gavin operating to the north of the regional city of Rennes and Guy to its south.

Meanwhile, Le Borgne and Dallow had teamed up with another *maquisard* called Deneville, who had been detached from a local group to the team. The team was also boosted by an additional member, twenty-two-year-old Maurice Miodon, a sergeant serving with No 4 (French) SAS, who had been inserted into France earlier that month as part of the SAS Operation Samwest but had since become separated from his unit. By now, Le Borgne had managed to visit the *département* chief of the FFI, Colonel Berthaud, and make contact with other leaders from the nearby towns of Scaer and Carhaix-Plouguer to arrange a *parachutage*. The drop zone identified was the same field near the village of Coray where Gilbert had been dropped on the same night as Francis, with the drop planned to take place in forty-eight hours.

It was late in the evening of 13 July when Ogden-Smith prepared to leave the farm to meet up again with his team. He was to be accompanied to the RV by two *maquisards*. One, Alexis Méfort, was an *agent de liaison* with the responsibility of liaising between *maquis* groups and locals in the area, particularly the farmers. The other was twenty-three-year-old Louis Fiche, a short and tanned Breton countryman. Fiche could speak excellent English. He was academically gifted but had been unable to continue with his studies because his elderly father needed help on the farm. He had first come to the attention of the *Maquis* at Quimperlé when he started making false identity cards and was now the leader of the section at Querrien.

Everyone at the farm at Lopers had gathered to see Ogden-Smith leave and to say goodbye. As he said his farewells he gave Jaouen's wife some money for sheltering him and Louis Kervédou remembers the *Major Anglais* taking his hand, looking him in the eye and telling him he would soon be back. Leaving a *maquisard* at the farm just in case the Germans had been watching the coming and going at Lopers, Alexis Méfort and Louis Fiche led Ogden-Smith away.

As the three men disappeared into the darkness, Le Duigou could not help but wonder what fate had in store for the *Major Anglais*. Many years after the war, as president of the National Union of Army Ex-Servicemen, René Le Duigou wrote a letter in response to an article he had seen about Ogden-Smith in a publication:

The major arrived at 5.00 a.m. tired and hungry near the village of Lopers, where he was taken in by L Jaouen, a friend of mine, who informed me at once that he had a foreigner in his home. I went immediately and recognised that he was a true English officer. At his own request I contacted the area's underground by radio transmitter, something which was easy and I was happy to do. The major was our guest for two days, the 12th and 13th July. He told me that he was 34 years old, married and the father of a six-month-old baby girl, and that a brother of his was a captain and prisoner and another was a senior NCO, and that after the war he would not remain in the army but would be a fisherman and he would like to come back here with his wife to enjoy fishing with us and so on. On the evening the major left us with the maquisards he was very pleasant talking with the women and children. After our last goodbye we saw the major going away to his fate and when we could not see him any longer we went to bed silently, feeling a gap within our group. Two days had been enough for the major to gain our trust and we would have sacrificed ourselves for him. He had come to give trust to the weak and bring arms to the stronger ones, many of whom were ex-servicemen of the 1914–18 war. All honour to you sir. We do not forget you.

Meanwhile, the rest of Francis had made their way to the village of Guiscriff where they were to meet up with Ogden-Smith but their arrival coincided with that of German troops. Le Borgne considered it unsafe to hang around and so they beat a hasty retreat. The reunion for Francis would have to wait, and with there being no chance of meeting up that night, Méfort and Fiche decided to take Ogden-Smith to Fiche's farm at Kerbozec.

CHAPTER SIX

Kerbozec

KERBOZEC IS SITUATED THREE miles to the south-west of the small town of Querrien and can be found just a few hundred yards along a narrow country lane that runs westwards from the small community of Belle Fontaine. In 1944 the farm was typical of many others in Brittany at the time. Its eleven hectares, with streams running through the farm from the nearby mill, the Moulin de Kerlévéné, presented a scene of tranquillity.

The farmland could be roughly apportioned as one-third natural prairie, one-third moorland and woods, and one-third arable, with a mix of wheat, oats, beets and potatoes. In the fields there were enough apple trees to produce an adequate supply of cider and on the slopes there were a mix of cherry trees and pear. Life at the farm was basic. The farmhouse, small with a slate roof, was in the style typical of many farms in Brittany. It had no electricity and cooking was done over an open fire. Water had to be gathered from the well and oil was rationed to one litre a month for lighting. Outside the farmhouse was a garden bordered by beautiful flowers, and amongst the farm buildings was a small cowshed with seven cows, a stable for two horses, a pigsty with a few pigs, with ten hens and a rooster roaming outside and a few rabbits here and there.

The farm was run by Louis Fiche's elderly father, also called Louis, who was seventy-one years old, and his mother, Marie-

Jeanne. She was sixteen years younger than her husband and she was helped by their daughter, Eliane, who was sixteen years old. The Fiche family was quite self-sufficient and all that needed buying was bread, salt, sugar and coffee. Their farm was just one of many in the area and neighbours helped each other with the work, such as planting and digging up potatoes, and sheaving and harvesting the wheat during harvest. While there was certainly hardship being under occupation, there were also times when people laughed and had fun. On Sundays the family harnessed the mare and went for a drive on the wagon or, from time to time, visited one of the families nearby as they all tried to continue their lives as best as they could.

The elderly Louis Fiche was almost totally deaf and of no concern to the Germans, but what they had seemingly failed to realise was that his son was an active member of the *Maquis* and his wife, too, provided food and shelter for *maquisards* whenever needed. Seventy years later, Eliane remembers: 'It was my mother who maintained ties with the *Maquis*.'

Much, but not all, of what went on at the farm involving the *Maquis* was kept from the elderly farmer. It was simply best that he did not know everything, although he was clearly aware of some of what went on at the farm. Marie-Jeanne and her son were also keen to keep Eliane out of danger. Neither of them wanted to think about the repercussions should she ever be taken in by the Germans for questioning, and so they kept as much as they could to themselves.

Marie-Jeanne was fully aware of the risks the family were taking. From what Eliane did know, she was also aware of the risks but all she longed for was for France to be free and to live the rest of her teenage years in freedom. Living under German occupation for so long had made her feel like she had said goodbye to her childhood; having a brother in the *Maquis*, and parents providing support, her views towards life had been hardened considerably. She was fully aware that *maquisards* were regularly tortured at Quimperlé and Le Faouët, and since the Allied landings she had noticed the change in attitude of the German soldiers in the area, many of whom seemed to realise that defeat was probably inevitable and had now decided to take out their anger on the local community. In Eliane's own words she recalls, 'It was horrible, adieu to my childhood.' Eliane knew that her family were determined to protect her from such a fate and so she fully understood why she was kept out of any conversations that would contain anything that would put her safety at risk.

Also staying at the farm during July 1944 was Marie-Jeanne's older brother, who was suffering from poor health, and Eliane's cousin, André Burbaud. André was thirteen years old and lived in Paris but he had been sent to the farm after the Allies had landed in Normandy – his family believing it would be safer for him in Brittany than in Paris. Eliane was pleased to have someone else closer to her own age to talk to.

It was late at night by the time Ogden-Smith, Méfort and Fiche arrived at Kerbozec. Marie-Jeanne had prepared a welcome supper in celebration of Ogden-Smith's arrival and they all sat down to *Gâteau Breton*, a speciality of Marie-Jeanne's which she kept for such special occasions, and English tea served in porcelain cups. It was a wonderful welcome.

It would soon be time to move on but for now they all enjoyed a wonderful evening together, talking about the war and optimistically looking forward to the liberation of France, which, surely, could now not be too far away. The young Louis Fiche and Ogden-Smith instantly got on very well together. In a letter written to Ogden-Smith's father after the war, Fiche wrote:

We were at once very good friends. Besides, it was impossible not to be. His natural kindness, his mirth, his perpetual smile did that, everybody who knew him became his friend.

It also turned out to be an unforgettable night for Eliane. She had been in bed in the next room when her brother, Méfort and Ogden-Smith had arrived at the farm but she was invited to join them all.

She would never forget the warmth of the *Major Anglais*. When it was finally time for the men to move on, Ogden-Smith took Eliane's hands in his and looked intently into her eyes, reassuring her that everything would be alright; it was just a brief moment in time but it was a moment Eliane would never forget. She then watched sadly as her brother, Méfort and Ogden-Smith slipped away under the cover of darkness. They were heading for the command post at Rosgrand Wood.

Finally, after four days of separation, Francis was together once more. Following the initial greetings there were the usual stories of what had happened to them since they had last seen each other on board the Liberator. There was so much to tell. Ogden-Smith talked about how he had survived on his own and then about Le Duigou and the Fiche family at Kerbozec, while Le Borgne and Dallow talked about the hospitality of André de Neuville, and the introduction of Deneville, Guyader and Miodon.

With Francis finally reunited, it was time to get some rest. The previous night had been exhausting but at least they were all back together and the team could get on with its work. It was now 14 July and the planned *parachutage* was just over twenty-four hours away. There was much to do.

The following morning the men of Francis were up early and moved north to make contact with another agent, a woman known as Rateau, who updated the team on what was happening further north. One of the Jed teams, Gilbert, needed a new radio set and, having found a suitable place to transmit, Dallow reported the news to London. Then during the evening, Francis and a large reception committee made the short journey to the DZ near the village of Coray to receive the drop.

They were expecting a drop of equipment and supplies from five aircraft to resupply the two *maquis* groups at Scaer and Guiscriff. Everything seemed to be going well but, unknown to Ogden-Smith, the Germans had discovered the DZ shortly after Gilbert had landed there five nights before. Gilbert had been lucky that night but since then the Germans had kept a close eye on the site, knowing that the *Maquis* would return.

Almost exactly on time the aircraft could be heard in the distance and the bonfires were lit to mark the DZ. One by one the aircraft made their approach. Ogden-Smith watched as dozens of parachutes could be made out against the moonlit sky as each aircraft made its drop. In the end there were only three aircraft, but nonetheless it was a large drop and the *maquisards* rushed from the trees to recover the equipment. It was then that the Germans struck. A large force from the garrison at Le Faouët, a mix of hardened German troops and pro-Nazi Russians, ambushed them. The fire fight that ensued was long and fierce, and it was only the arrival of further *maquis* groups that prevented a massacre, although at least twenty *maquisards* were killed. They had, however, managed to inflict heavy losses on the enemy. Francis had not stayed long after the fire fight had started and had quickly vacated the area – it was not their job to get involved in prolonged combat but it had been an extremely close call. Le Borgne later wrote:[25]

The drop on GUIDE [the DZ] was badly done. We never received Ops 1, 2 and 3 from London and we cannot realise how the people of Scaer could have been informed. The cargo of the first drop was not sufficient to arm the FTP. Three planes dropped their cargo and during the work collecting containers 300 enemy which had arrived from Le Faouët began to open fire. With the help of the Maquis, managed by some clever manoeuvring to get away. There were some heavy losses and contrary to our message, 24 patriots were killed, not 15, and the enemy 50 including 5 officers and they obtained 50 of the containers. With the rest of the armament we managed to equip a large FTP group and reinforced two other groups. We transported sufficient arms for 80 men at Bannalec where we had an unarmed group.

It had been a bad night and Ogden-Smith was left wondering just how the Germans had known where the DZ was located.

For a start, the Jeds had not received the normal pattern of radio communications from London. But had the Germans discovered the site after a previous drop or had they been informed? The only success to take away from the night was that enough equipment had been recovered before the fire fight had really taken hold.

All the Jed teams in the region now received word that a German sweep of the area was likely in an attempt to seek *maquis* groups and Allied special forces known to be operating in large numbers across the area. The Jeds were ordered to suspend active operations temporarily and move to a more hidden location.

With Francis now well away from the German troops, Ogden-Smith was keen to make contact with the two other Jed teams in the area, Giles and Gilbert. Giles, operating near Châteauneuf, was contactable by radio but Gilbert could only be contacted through the *Maquis*. He felt it important for the Jed teams to agree the geographic boundaries in which each team would operate so they would not get in each other's way and to avoid the risk of a potential engagement between the groups that each team was now working with. The plan agreed between the Jed team leaders was for Knox and his team Giles to remain to the north-west in the area of Châteauneuf-du-Faou and for Blathwayt and team Gilbert to remain in their current position further south and on the other side of Quimper. Ogden-Smith would take Francis back to Guiscriff where he would make contact with the local *maquis* group.

That night, Francis rested at a safe house in the village of Guiscriff. Ogden-Smith was now able to reflect on the past few days and he looked forward with optimism. On the positive side he was back with his team and they had even managed to increase its size to six. He was in good contact with London and his team had now made contact with the two other Jed teams in the area; they now had a plan to organise the *Maquis* in their area. However, the *parachutage* the previous night had been a disaster. Not only had most of the weapons and ammunition fallen into German hands but he knew that the Germans would now be hunting them down.

He was justifiably concerned because the following morning trucks of German troops arrived in the village. The trucks stopped right in front of the house where Ogden-Smith and his team were staying. There was no time to hang around and Francis was quickly on the move once more. By now they were well practiced at abandoning their position quickly, leaving as few signs as possible that they had been there at all.

Francis headed away from the village and towards Châteauneuf. During the afternoon they were able to make contact with a *maquis* group at Guiscriff led by a young French SAS officer, Lieutenant Gérard Gaultier de Carville. The two men talked at length and instantly got on well with each other. De Carville was just twenty years old and looked even younger. He had been born in St Arnaud and had escaped his home town of Brest in 1940 as German forces swept across France. Having later joined No 4 (French) SAS he had recently been parachuted into the Côtes-du-Nord as part of Operation Samwest and had been fortunate to escape with his life during heavy fighting at their base, after which he had become separated from his unit. He had since made contact with the *Maquis* and was now leading the local group.

13.   Gérard Gaultier de Carville of 4 (French) SAS was just twenty years old when he led the maquis group at Guiscriff. Ogden-Smith admired the outstanding courage and leadership of the young French officer and the two men got on extremely well during their short time together. De Carville died on 6 August 1944 after he was mortally wounded during heavy fighting in Rosporden, just a week after the death of Ogden-Smith. The two friends would eventually be buried alongside each other at the cemetery at Guiscriff.

Ogden-Smith then arranged to meet up with another *maquis* group at St Thois, but they arrived to find the group had moved on, although a handful of men had been left behind to warn them that their location was now known to the Germans. Unsurprisingly, Ogden-Smith decided not to hang around and he quickly moved his team on once more. Alexis Méfort was still with them and so he led the Jeds to a wood where they could safely hide. They were to make no radio contact with anyone. They could not afford to take the risk of having their radio transmissions detected nor could they take the risk of moving as a group. Ogden-Smith knew that his team were as safe as could be expected for the time being but they were now separated from the *Maquis*.

For the next two days Francis did not exist. They spent endless hours lying in thick gorse on soaking wet ground as German patrols passed nearby. The patrols were typically a dozen strong but were sometimes larger in numbers if the Germans had received a particular tip-off from one of the many collaborators in the area. The Jeds heard an occasional shot from the patrols as they attempted to unnerve anyone in hiding but this did not work. It was just a matter of remaining as calm as possible for the half an hour or so that it would take for the patrol to pass through their area, although they always hoped the patrol had not brought any dogs. At times the patrols passed within feet and the Jeds would have to hold their breath, or to breathe as shallow as possible – it was always a relief if the Germans were talking as they passed through because then they would not detect any sounds or signs of breathing.

Many things would have gone through Ogden-Smith's mind during those two days in hiding. They had to remain quiet and they could only converse through whispering when they thought it safe to do so. One thing that would have no doubt bothered Ogden-Smith was why the Germans had come to Guiscriff just hours after the Jeds had arrived? Was it a coincidence or did the Germans know they were there? If they did know that someone was there then who were they after – was it the *Maquis* or the Jeds? If it was the *Maquis* then it was best for the Jeds to be out of the way at that moment of time. Their responsibility was to all the groups in the area and not just one group at Guiscriff, no matter how good they were. Equally, if the Germans were looking for the Jeds then it was best for them to keep well away from the villages and farms. Either way, at this moment in time it was best for the Jeds and the *Maquis* to deal with the situation in their own way.

While Francis remained in hiding, Giles had been on the move to keep ahead of the increased German activity in the area. Giles had managed to receive a message informing them of the arrival of nine more men into the region: teams Hilary and Horace plus three liaison officers of the FFI. These men were to be met by Giles and then transported up to the north-west corner of western Brittany, and even further north than where Frederick was operating. The night after the insertion of Hilary and Horace, team Gerald was inserted into the southern part of Morbihan to operate with, but independently from, No 4 (French) SAS in support of Operation Dingson. Team Gerald would bring the number of Jed teams now operating in Brittany to eleven. Giles had also become aware of a German raid on Frederick's command post, which had resulted in the loss of the team's radio set and so Giles sent a message to London requesting the drop of a new radio as soon as possible and to alert the headquarters so they could cancel any planned use of DZs that had been identified by team Frederick, on the assumption that the location of any sites was now in German hands.

Late in their second day of hiding, Ogden-Smith considered it safe enough to move on and decided to make contact with Giles. Having successfully established contact, Francis left the wood to meet up with Giles at their hide at St Thois where Knox and Ogden-Smith discussed the options and agreed a new plan. Francis would head back towards Quimperlé, while Giles would move to Plessis. Ogden-Smith then managed to resume contact with de Carville and briefed him on the plan.

By the morning of 20 July German activity in the area seemed to have quietened down, or at least moved to a different area, and it was now time to get back to business. Francis left St Thois on bicycles acquired from de Carville's group and headed off towards Quimperlé. Just a few miles after setting off they were spotted by some *Feldgendarmes*, the German military police, in a car. The Germans immediately opened fire but the exchange of shots lasted only a few seconds and was soon over as Francis made their escape into the dense woodland on foot. Le Borgne later wrote:[26]

Left by cycle for Quimperlé as a team of six. 5 km after St Thois crossing the Chateauneuf-Quimper road we came face to face with some feldgendarmes in a car and empty truck. We exchanged a few shots killing a feldgendarme which made the remainder retire. We continued on foot.

The men of Francis had escaped unscathed but their brief exchange with the *Feldgendarmes* had again alerted the Germans of their position. Having covered as much distance as possible away from the scene, Francis spent the next day in hiding once again. It was simply not safe to move around, particularly by day, and so they found a suitable place deep in dense woodland where they could lie low for twenty-four hours or so. It gave the men a chance to rest once more and to assess what they had achieved during their twelve days behind enemy lines. It had been a difficult start, and hard work since, but Ogden-Smith felt that progress was being made. He also realised the Germans were continuously on their heels but he was satisfied that the Jeds had always managed to stay one step ahead. He also knew they could not stay in hiding too long because another *parachutage* was due to take place very soon.

By the time Ogden-Smith met up with de Carville again the following day he found the group had already received a large supply of arms and ammunition from a successful drop only the night before. There was now enough equipment to supply his group of 300 men, which meant that he could spread his three sections over an area of several miles, where they could have a much greater impact.

Ogden-Smith admired the leadership of the young de Carville and his appreciation of the tactical situation on the ground. He knew that he would certainly be able to rely on his group but there were still more groups in the area that needed to be more heavily armed. However, even if it was possible to arm all the groups, then it would only bring on a different problem, as he had already seen elsewhere in the area. Jed teams dropped into the region before his own had already tried to establish some control over *maquis* operations in their area, but the reality had been somewhat different as they were unable to prevent some of the smaller groups operating autonomously. While this was understandable up to a point, these attacks would often prove inefficient in terms of the resources used, and had at times resulted in unnecessary reprisals.

Francis was now a team of five as Deneville had returned to his section, although sadly he would be found dead some days later. German activity had now increased to another level as *Feldgendarmerie* units continued to hunt for the Jeds. The biggest threat came from 609 Feldgendarmerie de Quimperlé, led by Oberleutnant Lorenz Diebold. His unit consisted of twenty-seven non-commissioned officers and men and their role was to find *maquis* groups and to hunt down any special forces operating in the area. The unit had a fearsome reputation amongst the local French communities and some of the non-commissioned officers in particular were known to have shown no mercy when it came to dealing with the *Maquis* or any individuals suspected of sheltering any groups.

Blathwayt decided to relocate Gilbert to a position north of Quimper, and then to the north-west of Coray where his team could become more active with one *maquis* group in that area. Having been able to maintain communications with Dallow for the past ten days there was now the risk that Gilbert would lose touch with Francis altogether. Blathwayt was keen to make sure this did not happen because he knew that a signal was due to be transmitted from London in about ten days that would signal to the Jeds and *maquis* groups in the region to commence all-out guerrilla warfare against the enemy.

To keep safe meant to keep moving and not to spend more than forty-eight hours in one location. As Ogden-Smith contemplated when and where the next *parachutage* should take place, the team spent the next few days on the move. The terrain in western Brittany is undulating and in places quite rugged and harsh, particularly around Querrien in the central part of the area, where there is a mix of steep ravines and gulleys, as well as large forests and dense woodland. In the less-rugged areas the pastureland is divided into small hedged fields interspersed with groves of trees, known as *bocage*, and during the summer the crops in many of the fields are high. The surrounding embankments of earth and shrubbery, up to ten feet high in places, and at times embedded with trees, offer suitable concealment and protection.

For the Jeds this all helped them not being seen but at the same time meant that moving around was never easy and at times was very slow, particularly when carrying equipment. The team was able to move quicker across areas where there were cultivated fields or along the old narrow lanes but this could often be highly risky, even at night, and so the team tended to keep to the safety of the dense woodland and forests as much as possible. The towns were avoided, particularly Le Faouët and Quimperlé where the Germans were garrisoned, as was the road connecting the two, and even the smaller towns, such as Scaer and Querrien, were avoided because they were used by the Germans for accommodation and were regularly visited by the patrols.

Carrying as little equipment as possible, Ogden-Smith and his team generally moved at night, using the additional cover of woods. They tended to set up sites during the day in areas of rugged pasture, well away from any roads, with tall and thick prickly gorse to provide concealment from either passing German patrols or from overhead. No tents or shelters were erected but the Jeds instead chose to sleep in barns or cowsheds and sometimes ditches, using only blankets to provide any warmth or protection from the ground that had become soaked during what had been one of the wettest summers in living memory. Whenever it was thought safe to do so, the Jeds would take shelter in a farm outbuilding or in a derelict or disused cottage in the more remote areas but this was often considered to be high risk.

One of the farms considered safe enough was Fornigou, between Scaer and Guiscriff, which belonged to Francis Le Quéré, It was a large farm of some seventy hectares, which Le Quéré managed with his wife Rosine and their two children: fifteen-year-old Denise and seven-year-old Pierre. The farm was well known to Miodon, as *maquisards* were regular visitors when in the area, and so it was considered a safe enough location for Francis to visit. Nearly seventy years on Denise recalls: 'The team rested and ate in the cowshed. From there Dallow was able to make his radio calls to the other groups in the area and maintain contact with London.' For Dallow, it was an ideal location because the reception in the area was sufficiently strong enough for him to transmit and receive messages.

By the evening of 24 July, the men of Francis were back at their command post at Rosgrand near Quimperlé. The supply of arms and ammunition was going well in Zone A. At Carhaix there were enough arms for about 500 *maquisards* and the situation was similar for the group at Scaer; with de Carville's group at Guiscriff, well over a thousand were now armed. However, the situation in Zone B was quite different. So far, only about 200 in the zone were armed and so Ogden-Smith decided to focus the team's effort over the next few days to strengthening *maquis* groups nearer the Atlantic coast. The Americans were now breaking out of Normandy and advancing west towards Brest and south-westwards towards the Atlantic ports at Lorient and Saint Nazaire, and Ogden-Smith knew that the first *maquis* groups to join up with the Americans would be well armed. He also knew that it would be the Atlantic ports that would be heavily defended by the Germans and so there was still much to be done. Furthermore, there had been no drop for a while and so Dallow contacted London.

The next *parachutage* was arranged for the following night, with the first drop planned to take place at Bannalec and a second drop near Pont Aven in the centre of Zone B, situated on the Atlantic coastline to the north-west of Lorient. Coastal drops were far from ideal. There was not only the direction of run-in for the aircraft and the coastal winds to consider, but there was also the escape route to think about for the reception committee – should they be ambushed, they would be penned in against the sea and it would restrict their chance of escape.

Francis had gone to meet the drop at Bannalec but although the reception committee were in place in good time the drop could not take place. The aircraft were late and did not arrive in the area until it was nearly dawn, by which time there was a large presence of German troops in the area. Ogden-Smith had heard the aircraft approaching the DZ but had decided against having the bonfires lit: it was too risky and would most likely have ended in carnage. The drop had not taken place, although the aircraft had circled in the vicinity for a short period of time before they headed off towards the coast.

At the second DZ near Pont Aven the situation had been much the same, although the drop did take place. The reception committee had been in place in good time but it was dawn by the time the aircraft arrived and because it was getting light there had been insufficient time to get all of the equipment away. All the reception committee could do was to conceal the containers as best they could with the intention of returning the following day, or even in a couple of days, to recover the arms and ammunition. However, concealing a large number of containers quickly was never easy. The Germans knew that a drop had taken place and although they had not managed to discover the DZ in time to capture anyone from the *Maquis* they conducted a thorough search of the area the following day and soon discovered the containers, barely concealed in the fresh soil. Everything the *maquisards* had left behind was discovered. It had been another bad night. Le Borgne later summed up the frustrations of the night:[27]

> An unlucky drop at Pont Aven in the centre of Zone B. The planes arrived at dawn. Distribution of arms a long job, which cannot be undertaken. Containers are hidden but discovered during the morning by the Boche who took away the arms for 300 men. At Bannalec a drop had to be cancelled owing to troop movements. We saw our planes but did not light up for them. After these two unlucky attempts we decided to cease all drops in Zone B and leave them any accessories from Zone A.

As Ogden-Smith led his team back towards Quimperlé he discovered that German reinforcements, totalling some 600 men, had now arrived in the town. Considering it was unsafe to return to their command post, he led Francis back towards Bannalec. Dallow had been in occasional contact with Norman Wood of Gilbert, who was still waiting for his replacement radios, but the two men were now close enough to establish good contact. Gilbert was at a site just a few miles to the north-west of Coray and had met up with a well organised group in the area. Ogden-Smith now saw the opportunity to provide Gilbert with its first *parachutage* and so arranged for Gilbert to receive a drop that night. Once back at a safe hide near Bannalec, Dallow received a message confirming that an aircraft would be sent and that more containers were to be dropped that night.

Later that night, to the north, Gilbert waited patiently at the DZ near Coray. It had seemed ages since they had first parachuted into France and now they waited for their first drop. As the aircraft approached the DZ the bonfires were lit and the aircraft made its drop as planned but Germans in the area had clearly been tipped off. Fighting broke out immediately but Gilbert and the reception committee managed to hold off the Germans for long enough while the *maquisards* managed to get away with about one-third of the equipment from the drop, although the rest was lost.

The following day Dallow contacted London once more. Francis had already identified another DZ to the south-west of Coray and so Dallow once again relayed a message to Gilbert to expect another *parachutage* that night. This time the drop proved to be successful and Gilbert received the replacement radio set that it had long been waiting for.

The following day, 28 July, the Germans conducted a search just to the north of Quimperlé and surprised a *maquis* group of around fifty men in the small village of Tremeven. After the heavy fighting had finished, during which two of the group and five Germans were killed, ten containers were seized, albeit empty ones at that stage – although the radio set that had been dropped for Giles the previous day had now fallen into enemy hands.

The noose was now tightening for the Jeds. That same day the Germans intensified their search once more and began rounding up *maquis* leaders in the area. Having surrounded the home of André de Neuville for eight hours they eventually arrested an elderly retired French army general, Louis Marie Joseph de Torquat de la Coulerie, and a known member of the *Maquis*, André Hervé. The Germans believed Général de Torquat was the head of *maquis* groups in the area and so they took him to the prison at Quimperlé for questioning. Although de Neuville was not captured during the day, he did return to the château that evening with the intention of recovering some of Francis's equipment as well as a radio left behind at their command post. Unfortunately, the Germans were waiting for him and, as he tried to make his escape, André de Neuville was gunned down in Rosgrand Wood. Général de Torquat would not survive much longer. Along with twenty *maquisards*, he was executed two days later; he was seventy-five years old.

There was seemingly no end to the atrocities. As the Allies advanced towards the area, the Germans stopped at nothing during the final weeks of occupation to wipe out those who they believed were members of the *Maquis*. They burned farms and carried out atrocities against the French farmers if any of them were suspected of hiding or providing shelter for the *Maquis* or Jeds. In Le Faouët alone, where the Germans used the school, École Sainte-Barbe, as a prison and court, seventy French men were condemned to death in the last two months of the German occupation during June and July 1944. The appalling pattern for those unfortunate enough to be captured was much the same. First they were held captive before each man was then tried by the Germans, after which they were executed at first light the following morning at a remote location in the surrounding countryside – far enough away from the towns and villages so that the execution could not be seen, but they were usually always heard.

Ogden-Smith now decided to take his team well out of the way and further north, to the market town of Carhaix to wait for the next *parachutage*. He also knew from a previous meeting with a *maquisard* from the town, Yvres Riou, that the team could lie up for a couple of days until the situation around Quimperlé had calmed down.

Travelling on foot to avoid the roads and tracks in the area, Ogden-Smith would have pondered over the situation. Like the other Jed team leaders, he was fully aware that a signal would soon be sent from London directing the commencement of open guerrilla warfare against the German forces still in occupied France. If the *Maquis* was to create as much havoc as possible and incur maximum losses amongst German forces in Brittany then it was essential that more arms and ammunition were dropped into France. In the whole region he reckoned there were now some 3,000 *maquisards* armed and a further drop planned for the following night by six aircraft would resupply two groups at Carhaix and Bannalec.

During the night Ogden-Smith decided to rest his team at Kerbozec. They had managed to get a lift to the farm by Alexis Méfort and the young Louis Fiche. With more and more German troops known to be sweeping the area, the day of 29 July was spent in hiding. The elderly farmer Louis Fiche and his wife Marie-Jeanne had left the farm by bicycle early that morning to attend a family funeral at Bannalec. It was a journey of several miles and they would be gone many hours.

Eliane had been left to look after the house while André had gone to play with the miller's son and look after the cows; the boys were of similar age and got on well together. Eliane had good company that day. Guy Savin, a nineteen-year-old student and a friend of the younger Louis Fiche, was also staying at the farm, as were two of his friends, Lulu Py, aged sixteen, and another teenage boy called Jean Sinquin. The three boys had all been staying at the farm and sleeping on straw in the loft. Guy's mother, Marie-Henriette, was also at the farm. She had come to visit the family the previous day to see where her son was staying and had decided to stop over herself. During the afternoon, a few *maquisards*, led by twenty-five-year-old Albert Norvez, had also arrived at the farm, although only one or two of them were armed. Everyone had been chatting together and having fun. Some had even gone down to the hide.

The past few days had been such good fun with so much company around the farm, and news of the Allied advance had brought a lot of hope and optimism. With so many visitors at Kerbozec, Marie-Jeanne had been keen to get back to the farm as soon as she could and, returning later in the day, she and Eliane prepared food for everyone while her husband went off to tend to the cows and the younger Louis Fiche went off to find some bicycles for the team in preparation for the *parachutage* later that night.

Once Marie-Jeanne had prepared the food, including another *Gâteau Breton* for her visitors, the *maquisards* made their way to the farmhouse. At 8.00 p.m. the food was ready. While the rest gathered to eat at the farmhouse, the five members of Francis, including Guyader and Miodon, were left hiding in a ditch, little more than a hundred yards away.

Ogden-Smith again surveyed their position. Although the ditch was barely wide enough or deep enough to completely conceal their position, it was overhung by trees and a hedge of brambles on one side, marking the boundary of the agricultural field that lay between Francis and the farmhouse, which offered them some protection and concealment on that side. Looking up the gentle slope of the field he could clearly see the farmhouse and looking to his right he noted that the wooded land was higher: any threat would probably come from that direction but he knew it would soon be dark.

He could not fail to admire the beauty of the location, with its dense woodland looking as if it had never been touched by human hand, an area of reeds where a trout stream once flowed and the mill at Moulin de Kerlévéné nearby. It had been a beautiful warm summer's day and the sun was only just starting to go down. At any time other than this, the whole setting would have represented a perfectly natural early evening country scene in north-west France but the whole situation was about to take a nasty turn.

It was around 8.30 p.m. when the Jeds received a sudden warning that Germans were approaching, but no sooner had the alarm been raised than the sound of trucks could be heard approaching in the distance. Inside the farmhouse the trucks had also been heard – with no way of helping Francis, the *maquisards* quickly made their escape. As things were to turn out, there was nothing they could have done.

With the lookout now gone, Ogden-Smith was blind to what was happening up on the road. What the men of Francis could not see were two trucks approaching Kerbozec. The trucks were full with fifteen *Feldgendarmes* from Quimperlé, led by Oberfeldwebel Walter Rubsam, accompanied by nearly sixty soldiers of the Wehrmacht. The trucks stopped short of the farm, near a track that led towards the Moulin de Kerlévéné.

Inside the mill, fifty-two-year-old François Naour, his wife and his thirteen-year-old son Yves had also heard the trucks and were now observing the scene. They could see the German soldiers in their camouflaged battle dress as they quietly made their way up the track towards the mill. They then watched the Germans take up their positions on the higher ground to the east of the farm, looking down towards where, unbeknown to the miller and his family, the members of Francis were in hiding just a hundred yards or so away. Naour then watched in fear as three Germans continued up to the mill; they took him out into the courtyard, where he was placed under guard.

Not only did the Germans know that the five members of Francis were at the farm, they also knew exactly where the hide was located. Heavily outnumbered and occupying the lower ground, Francis would stand little chance.

Meanwhile, in the hide, Ogden-Smith had watched a German staff car approach the farm. It stopped outside and in the back he could see a Wehrmacht officer with a woman companion. He instantly knew they were in trouble. For a brief moment he hoped the car would move on so that his team could make their escape but this time they were not to be so lucky. The German officer got out of the car and slowly walked down the track from the farmhouse towards where they were hiding. Ogden-Smith could now see two other Germans making their way quickly towards them and a third was seen moving quickly, parallel to the track, in an attempt to outflank them from the north-east.

For Francis, their luck had finally run out. They had to get out of there as quickly as possible. Dallow was the first to move. He immediately picked up the radio receiver, transmitter and his carbine and scarpered quickly down the ditch, followed by Guyader. Shots were fired straight away – they had been spotted.

The rest of Francis had been quick to respond and opened fire on the Germans. By now Dallow had managed to put enough distance between him and the Germans but he knew there was little or no chance of getting away. After covering about fifty yards along the ditch he decided to mount the bank to try and make his escape through the adjoining field but on reaching the top of the bank he slipped and fell into the ferns and a thick bush of brambles next to a tree. Dallow could hear the firing behind him, which was now getting more intense, and could see the radio transmitter and his carbine laying just two yards away. While his first thought was that he was trapped, and was now doomed to some horrible fate, it was a touch of fortune that was ultimately to save his life. Dallow would somehow remain unseen, helped because of the other events that were happening at the same time, which meant the eyes of the *Feldgendarmes* were clearly focused elsewhere. Having realised that he had so far remained unseen, and that his position was seemingly concealed by bracken and brambles, Dallow knew that his only chance of survival was to remain hidden.

Meanwhile, Guyader had managed to get further along the ditch than Dallow before he was hit. The force of the bullet impacting his body had spun him round and he stumbled on a few yards before collapsing into the water-filled ditch. Because he had been shot from an angle above, the bullet hit him between the shoulder and neck and had passed through his body and exited lower down by his hip. Guyader was lucky to be alive but he was convinced he was about to die. He was wounded, although not fatally, but he felt it would only be a matter of time before the Germans found him, after which they would surely finish him off. He was aware of further shots being fired somewhere behind him but for now he was alive, although he felt too weak to make any further escape and so all he could do was hope that he remained unseen.

While Dallow and Guyader had tried to make their escape, the German officer had continued further down the farm track. He had clearly seen Guyader trying to make his escape just a matter of yards away but just at that moment Le Borgne appeared. The German officer was startled. He had not spotted the Frenchman until now and hastily opened fire without taking aim. It was a mistake that was to cost the German officer his life. Le Borgne had been trained well and using a technique known amongst the French as a 'Roule-Boule', Le Borgne rolled forward and emptied four rounds in quick succession into the German, killing him instantly.

As Le Borgne was making his escape, and Dallow and Guyader were lying silently and unobserved further up the ditch, all three men could still hear the sound of gunfire coming from further back down the ditch, where Ogden-Smith and Miodon remained. Inside the farmhouse Eliane also listened to the awful sound – not only the horrendous sound of gunfire but also the unforgettable sound of the wounded and the dying. As the gunfire continued, the fight was clearly not yet over but she feared the worst.

Ogden-Smith now started to make his escape but he could see how desperate the situation had become. He used the water-filled ditch to get as much cover as he could but it was no good. He had been spotted and any chance of making his escape had gone.

The heroic action of Colin Ogden-Smith and Maurice Miodon during the final and fateful moments that followed at Kerbozec would never be forgotten by those who were there and the memories of their personal sacrifice so that others might live would remain with the people of Querrien for generations to come. Two men, a British officer and a French sergeant, who barely knew each other having only recently met, were now fighting side by side for the liberation of France and were very soon to die together.

For what must have seemed like an eternity, the two men kept the Germans at bay; each minute that passed meant the others could hopefully get further away. Finally, Ogden-Smith decided to make a break for it but as he tried to leave the ditch to climb over a hedge he was hit in the stomach by a burst of machine-gun fire and fell back against the base of a tree. Badly wounded he did not have the strength to get away. He reached for his morphine to relieve the pain and then started to apply a bandage in an attempt to stop the bleeding. Many things would have gone through Ogden-Smith's mind during those final minutes. He was now bleeding profusely from his stomach but he knew the Germans would show him no mercy, even though he was in uniform and was badly wounded. Besides, even if they did take him prisoner, he knew exactly what awaited him.

Miodon was just a few yards from Ogden-Smith and had been wounded during the opening exchanges when a grenade had exploded close to him. He had been caught almost fully in the blast, fragments shattering his leg and arm. The young and fearless Frenchman, now badly wounded, dragged himself out from his cover and into the face of the Germans. He then braced himself and kept up covering fire, first with his carbine and then when his ammunition had run out he kept firing with his pistol. His last words could be clearly heard as he shouted to the Germans, 'You need not be afraid, I have got no more ammunition.'

By now several Germans had swooped on their helpless prey. Many of their colleagues lay dead or wounded in the field and they clearly sought revenge. Ogden-Smith was unable to move. His wound to the stomach had caused him considerable pain but the massive dose of morphine was now taking effect. As the pain eased, his life slowly ebbed away. Moments later the heroic Colin Ogden-Smith was dead, his gun empty and ammunition cases lying all around.

The fight was over. It had lasted forty-five minutes. The body of Ogden-Smith and the mortally wounded Miodon lay at the point where each had fallen. The Germans approached the Frenchman cautiously and ordered him to put his hands up. Miodon was helpless but the German response would be as callous as all that had gone before.

Meanwhile, in a field further away, the elderly farmer, Louis Fiche, had been tending to his cows when the Germans had arrived at his farm and they now turned on him. Fiche was more than a hundred yards away from where the fighting had taken place but the sudden arrival of the German soldiers, combined with the elderly French farmer's difficulty in hearing, all added to the confusion for the helpless Fiche. Then, in what can only be described as a barbaric act, the Germans took the elderly farmer and killed him as an atrocious act of reprisal by bayoneting him in the back and shooting him in the chest.

Back at the Moulin de Kerlévéné, Naour had remained under guard and had heard all that had happened down on the farm. With the fighting over he was then led down to the field where he could see the shapes of two men on the ground, surrounded by German soldiers. As he got closer he could see that one man was dead and recognised his uniform as a British officer. Ogden-Smith was lying on his back, his uniform soaked from the water in the stream and the cause of death was obvious. One of the soldiers turned him over so that he was lying face down. Naour looked on saddened as one of the Germans searched Ogden-Smith and removed his machine gun, torch, identity card and other papers, and finally his personal belongings.

Naour noticed two *Feldgendarmes* standing nearby and watching over the proceedings. The light was now fading but he could see that one was a tall, slender-looking man with a lean face and greyish hair, aged somewhere in his early forties. The other was not so tall and a few years younger, probably in his thirties, but was clearly in charge of the group. Having found the money contained in Ogden-Smith's belt, the Germans eagerly spread their booty amongst themselves. They then used their bayonets to cut off the buttons and rank insignia from his uniform as souvenirs before a soldier handed over Ogden-Smith's wallet and other personal belongings to the smaller of the two *Feldgendarmes*. Naour then observed what can only be described as an atrocious act by one of the soldiers: it was an act that would become the subject of a war crimes investigation after the war.

Naour could also see the Frenchman lying wounded nearby. One of the German soldiers wanted to finish Miodon off with his machine gun but the *Feldgendarme* in charge would not allow him to do so. The taller of the two *Feldgendarmes* could speak French and explained to Naour that he was to be taken to Quimperlé for interrogation by his senior colleague. As Naour was led off towards the farmhouse he passed within five yards of Miodon and noticed the young Frenchman was still alive. He had not got very far past Miodon when he heard shots behind him. Convinced that he was the intended target, Naour turned round. The bullets had not been for him but he could see that more Germans were now gathered around Miodon, including the two *Feldgendarmes*. The gallant young Frenchman was dead. Naour was then told to leave the farm quickly. He did not wait to be told twice.

While most of the Germans had been dealing with events outside, two had stormed into the farmhouse when they had first arrived at Kerbozec. Picking on Marie-Jeanne, they wanted to know who was out on the farm – she, of course, denied any knowledge of anyone or anything. They were then given just ten minutes to leave the house, taking with them whatever they could carry. They quickly gathered some clothes and bedding before moving outside. They did not know the full extent of what was going on outside but they knew the situation was bad. In Eliane's own words many years later, she said: 'The noise we heard from the farmhouse was so terrible. There was a mixture of sounds. There was the firing, although I could not distinguish between the guns, but mainly it was the crying of the wounded and dying that affected me most.'

Although the Germans had spared the lives of those inside the farmhouse, they showed no other compassion for those at Kerbozec. First they ransacked and looted the house and they then set about brutally killing the farm animals in the yard before taking some of them away. It was carnage. The Germans then set fire to the farmhouse in yet another appalling act of vengeance. Eliane recalls, the sadness still evident in her voice and eyes, 'Before the house was set alight my mother and I fetched sheets and blankets from our home, and then watched its destruction. The pigsty and stable were not burnt and so we at least had a roof!'

After the events had concluded across the farm, many of the Germans stood around outside, laughing and joking as the farmhouse burned. As they were leaving they told Marie-Jeanne and Eliane that there were dead bodies out on the farm and they were not to be touched. Finally, the Germans left. It was around

11.00 p.m. when the *Feldgendarmes* arrived back at Quimperlé. In his report to his commanding officer, Rubsam simply informed Diebold that his unit had come under attack from the farmhouse and they had then dealt with the situation, during which one *Feldgendarme* had been killed.

Meanwhile back at Kerbozec the survivors took up refuge in the pig sty and stable. They were now concerned for the whereabouts and safety of everyone, including the elderly Louis Fiche who had not returned. For Eliane it was a terrible night. The farmhouse was still burning.

CHAPTER SEVEN

After Kerbozec

DAYBREAK ON THE MORNING of 30 July revealed a scene of utter devastation at Kerbozec. It was far from the tranquil Sunday morning scene in Brittany that it should have been. The farmhouse was burned out and there was nothing left to salvage inside. The old clock over the fire had stopped at a quarter to nine, marking the time the carnage inside the farmhouse had first started.

Eliane had now learned from her mother that her father was dead; she had found his body in a field. Later that morning the local French doctor, Emile-Jean Auffret, arrived to examine the corpses. Marie-Jeanne and Eliane were present: it was an awful task, after which Marie-Jeanne covered each body with some sheets. It was all that she could do. The Germans now returned to the farm, accompanied by the mayor, Alexis Rannou, and a few others. The French were forbidden from taking the bodies to the cemetery and so all three were buried in shallow graves on the farm. The body of Louis Fiche was carried the 300 yards or so to be buried in one shallow grave with Ogden-Smith; they were buried side by side just a few yards from the tree where Ogden-Smith had died. Miodon was buried nearby in a ditch close to where he had been killed. Marie-Jeanne later made three crosses, one each for the three fallen heroes, and placed each at the place where they had died.

There can be some comfort in the fact that Ogden-Smith's and Miodon's deaths had not been in vain. The French radio assistant, Guyader, had been lucky to have remained undiscovered after the fighting was over. For four hours he hid on the edge of the ditch, half in water and half out, drifting in and out of consciousness. Although badly wounded, he waited until the Germans had gone before making his move under the cover of darkness. Deciding that it would be safer to proceed unarmed, in case he should be stopped and searched, Guyader discarded his weapons. He had enough strength to crawl out of the ditch and then headed off across the meadow before crossing a small river and eventually coming across a small house, which he knew to be empty, where he found some clothes and quickly changed. Knowing that it would be unsafe to stay at the house, he moved on once more. As dawn broke he hid under a large overhanging stone next to the river before later moving on again. He had kept heading south towards Quimperlé, where he knew he could get medical help and would be safe. He considered it too dangerous to use the roads in case a passing German patrol stopped him and noticed his wounds, and so he kept to the fields and wooded areas for cover. Twice he stopped at houses but on both occasions the terrified occupants were too frightened to help. By now it was late morning and Guyader, having struggled for some six miles or more, was tired, hungry and in a lot of pain. Close to the village of Mellac, just to the north of Quimperlé, he rested in a ditch and fell asleep. Being a nice Sunday morning, a local woman was out walking along the same narrow road with her little boy. She could hear something stirring nearby and as she got closer she saw the Frenchman in the ditch. She then raised help and soon after, Guyader was taken by a *maquisard* to the hospital in Quimperlé. With a suitable cover story he was safe at last.

Guy Le Borgne had managed to make his escape during the confusion of the fire fight. After killing the German officer he escaped southwards, passing to the west of the mill, and under the cover of darkness made his way northwards towards Guiscriff. Lying low the following day he then continued his journey at night. When a farmer came across him resting in a field, he said, 'Don't be afraid, I am French. I am trying to join up with the *Maquis* at Guiscriff.'

The farmer fed him and provided him with shelter and then set off on his bike to inform the *Maquis*. That night several people arrived at the farm. The children were sent off to bed and the farmer's wife made a large onion omelette with potatoes for her guests. Le Borgne had met up with de Carville once again.

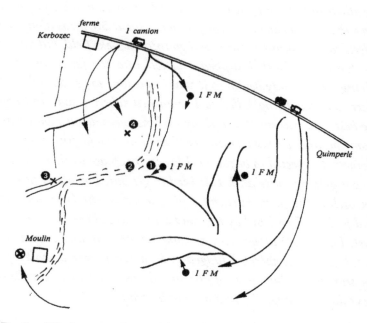

14. The Battle of Kerbozec as drawn by Guy Le Borgne and Barthélémy Guyader. Clearly marked are the positions of the staff car at the farm house (ferme) and where the two trucks pulled up along the narrow country lane leading to Kerbozec. The flanking manoeuvres of the German troops and feldgendarmes are shown by the arrows and Moulin is the mill. The numbers show: 1 – position where Ogden-Smith was killed; 2 – Dallow's position where he lay in hiding after trying to escape along the ditch; 3 – Guyader's position further along the ditch where he remained wounded and in hiding; 4 – position where Miodon was killed. Le Borgne's escape route is marked by a dashed line running along the ditch.

At that stage Le Borgne had no idea what had happened to Ogden-Smith and Dallow, but feared the worst for them both. However, Dallow was alive and well. He had been incredibly fortunate to have remained undiscovered. Frightened for his life he had remained hidden in the bracken and brambles where he fell. He later wrote:[28]

We received the alarm that the Germans were coming and at the same time heard the German lorries. Immediately I picked up the receiver, transmitter and my carbine and began to run with two patriots along the ditch but it was rather awkward with so much equipment so I gave the receiver to one of the patriots. About 50 yards along the ditch I decided to mount the bank and go into the next field, but on reaching the top of the bank I slipped and fell into the ferns and brambles. Firing had already begun so it was impossible to get out of my 'hiding place' without being killed so I remained where I was and hoped for the best. The transmitter and my carbine were about two yards away from me and I was certain the Germans would find them. At any moment I expected to be found. I lay in this place until 11 p.m. and as it was getting quite dark I decided to get out. For about five minutes I watched the farm burning and listened to the Germans laughing and joking. Then I hid by the road and watched the German trucks go past. I was now alone with no compass, no map and only a .45 Colt, so taking course which I judged to be north I started walking. I saw the stars twice during the night and altered my course accordingly. The next day I managed to find a maquis group.

After food and rest, Dallow was given shelter until everything had quietened down. On 31 July he was reunited with Le Borgne. By then, confirmation of Ogden-Smith's death had filtered through to the *Maquis* and came as awful news. Le Borgne knew there had been no time for Ogden-Smith to discard his maps and documents and Dallow had lost part of his radio, so Le Borgne instructed Gilbert to contact London to inform headquarters that Ogden-

Smith was dead and to assume the position of their DZs had now been compromised.

Fortunately the planned *parachutage* at Guiscriff that night, involving a large drop by six aircraft, was successful, after which the arms and equipment was distributed between the two groups at Carhaix and Bannalec. The signal expected from London for the *Maquis* to commence all out guerrilla warfare against the Germans was due in the next couple of days and so every effort was being made to drop as much arms and equipment as possible into the region.

The Germans were convinced they had captured vital information about the DZs and so the garrisons at Le Faouët and Scaer continued to conduct searches in the area from dawn to dusk. However, the way that information was recorded by Ogden-Smith on his maps and the information contained in the documents were not that obvious – Ogden-Smith, and all the other Jeds for that matter, knew that capture or death was always possible and so no man wanted to be responsible for giving vital information away to the enemy. Although there were five DZs and ten *maquis* groups operating within the area of Francis, the German searches proved fruitless. Nothing was found and no one was captured.

Le Borgne and Dallow then continued the mission of Francis. Quimperlé was liberated on 5 August, after which they joined up with Gilbert and Ronald for the battle of Quimper, where a strong German garrison was located. The group soon became involved in heavy fighting around the small town of Rosporden and, during a clash with a convoy of trucks, the valiant young Gérard Gaultier de Carville, the twenty-year-old SAS leader of the group at Guiscriff, was mortally wounded; he was rushed to a medical clinic in Quimper but died from his wounds on 6 August. De Carville was later awarded the Croix de Guerre and appointed a Chevalier de la Legion d'Honneur for his gallantry. Quimper was liberated on 8 August, after which Le Borgne and Dallow worked with the Aloès Mission, the infiltration of women into Lorient to obtain information on the strength of the German garrison and its intent. Hitler had designated all the Atlantic ports as fortresses to be defended to the last man, and so rather than risk more casualties at the port, the Americans simply surrounded Lorient for the rest of the war. The two Jeds were then sent to the small port of Douarnenez, to the north-west of Quimper, to commandeer ten vessels and organise 500 seamen to prevent the Germans from leaving the Crozen Peninsula and to take in more supplies at Raz Point. Finally, Le Borgne and Dallow were recalled to England. They made their way to Bénodet where, on 9 September, they boarded HMS *Minna*, a fishery protection vessel and one of many small craft used by the Admiralty: its typically French appearance made the *Minna* ideal for special operations. Two days later the two survivors of Francis arrived safely back in England. Their mission was over.

There would always come a point when the Jedburgh missions were considered completed and in October 1944 the order was given for all Jed teams still in France to return to England. By then, nearly 280 men had been parachuted into France as part of the Jedburgh programme. They had joined nearly 400 other SOE and OSS agents operating behind enemy lines, and a further 3,000 operating with various American operational groups or British SAS teams. The work of the Jeds and the other special forces in France was finished and the FFI would soon be absorbed into the French Army to fight alongside its Allies.

Back in England, Le Borgne and Dallow completed their reports.[29] Having assumed command of the team after the death of Ogden-Smith, Le Borgne was required to write a full report on the Francis mission, covering the events that had occurred from the time the team had first been dropped into France until their departure two months later. In the report Le Borgne highlighted the difficulties the team had experienced during the mission, particularly when it came to moving around, and made it clear that he felt the enemy often knew about where the drops were due to take place. He was, at times, critical about the lack of support the team had been given during their early weeks behind enemy lines.

With hindsight, most of Le Borgne's comments were fully justified, particularly those relating to equipment being dropped in the wrong place, but those back in London may have felt the team had asked for too much given the resources available to the SOE at the time; mortars and PIATs (a portable anti-tank weapon), for example, were never going to be easy to come by in the days following the Allied invasion when every infantry unit in the army was probably making the same request.

In his report, Le Borgne did pay tribute to the Jedset and the excellent work of the young radio operator Dallow, reporting that radio broadcasts had often been very difficult to receive and understand due to the atmospheric conditions in the area and because the Jeds had spent so much time on the move, particularly at night. Le Borgne was also keen to report the atrocities of the Germans against the French community, citing the burning of farms and the killing of a farmer as examples. He also reported in some detail their appalling acts against captured members of the *Maquis* where the wounded were killed rather than being taken as prisoners, often after suffering terrible torture first; in these acts he specifically mentioned the *Feldgendarmes* at Quimperlé. While he could not provide evidence of any torture carried out against captured Jeds, or any other Allied special forces for that matter, he reported the Germans had clearly decided not to take any prisoners but chose instead to kill in cold blood those they had captured, citing the deaths of Colin Ogden-Smith and Maurice Miodon. He also included his recollection of the events at Kerbozec on 29 July 1944:[30]

29th July at the farm of Kerbozec in the hamlet of Querrien, where the team FRANCIS plus SAS Maurice Miodon, the patriot Guyader were surrounded following treason by a detachment of approximately 100 feldgendarmes, which had come from Quimperlé. The Major and the SAS [Miodon] were seriously wounded at the start of the action.

Sgt Dallow managed to shelter for two hours in the actual scene of the battle and despite a German search was not found. The patriot Guyader although seriously wounded managed to hide in a stream for four hours and afterwards despite his wounds did 6 km on foot to find shelter. Having had the luck of killing the captain in charge of the operation, which caused a certain amount of confusion and which I managed to profit by, I escaped through the German lines. The Major, seriously wounded in the stomach by a burst of fire and unable to move, gave himself some morphia and applied first aid. He was deliberately shot by the Germans. The SAS, wounded by a grenade, dragged himself in front of the Germans in order to allow his comrades to retire. He fired four magazines, killing and wounding quite a number of the enemy. Being then out of ammunition he shouted to the Germans as follows: – 'you need not be afraid, I have got no more ammunition.' The Germans then approached and ordered hands up. They got hold of him, fired a burst of sub-machine gun into him and finished him off with a bullet in the temple. Major Ogden-Smith and Miodon were both in uniform and wore the insignia of their rank. The Germans burnt the farm, killed the farmer, a Mr Fiche, aged 72 years[31] with a bayonet in his back, took away all the farmer's goods and drove off the cattle. The Germans stole everything off the corpses in the way of jewellery, money, boots and effects.

At the end of his report he named two members of the Feldgendarmerie de Quimperlé deemed responsible for the events at the farm and concluded:

We were given away by a Belgian collaborator who lived a few kilometres from there and whilst walking in the country had seen us. He sent his wife to Quimperlé to inform the feldgendarmes, and it was her who was in the car leading the detachment to the spot. The Belgian, his wife and his eldest son were executed by my orders, by the patriots two days later.[32]

In his version of events, Dallow concluded:[33]

The SAS sergeant deliberately threw his life away, apparently in order to help us escape. He stayed behind and fired all his ammunition, he was then shot by the Germans. Major Ogden-Smith was killed trying to escape but it is almost certain he killed or wounded four Germans. He was first badly wounded and then instead of being taken prisoner he was shot through the head. The farmer who was an old man of 71 was killed by the bayonet.

Le Borgne was also keen to make sure that the sacrifice made by Ogden-Smith did not go unnoticed. Ogden-Smith was subsequently recommended for a posthumous Legion d'Honneur, his citation describing how he had been killed after his group had been betrayed and that Ogden-Smith had protected the retreat of others.[34] In a letter written to Ogden-Smith's mother from Paris, dated 14 December 1944, Guy Le Borgne wrote (in English):

I went into the Ministere de la Guerre for the decoration of Colin. They received my proposition but they said they must send firstly to the English headquarters, so they sent the proposition to our organisation. I sent a letter from here to the major who is in charge of the decorations and that I saw in London the day before I came and saw you in London. You will have now to wait but I think it will be long, perhaps some months.

Three days later, Le Borgne's mother also wrote to Ogden-Smith's mother:

My son, Guy Le Borgne, or perhaps you know him in the name of Zachmeur, told me how nice you were to him when he went to London, and for that I send you many thanks. My son told me that you unfortunately lost one of your sons in Brittany. I join you in your sorrow. Guy told me how nice Major Ogden-Smith was and how close he was to him during the campaign in Brittany. He was a great officer and believe me that the French people are full of admiration for those who came to liberate the land of Brittany and Normandy. I hope that all the sacrifices endured during that horrible war will help for a further victory and will again give the world long peace. I wish also you will soon see your son in Germany and that he comes home healthy, as well as your third son which I believe is also in the army. I wish you madam a lot of courage, because we know that the English people are strong enough to endure all the sacrifices.

Le Borgne's belief that Ogden-Smith's heroism and sacrifice should not go unnoticed was initially given support but ultimately nothing ever came of the recommendation. Ogden-Smith was, however, posthumously awarded a Mention in Despatches: it was the only British award he could realistically be considered for. Amongst the list of forty names listed in the *London Gazette* entry dated 7 June 1945 was: 91977 War Substantive Captain and Temporary Major Colin Malcolm Ogden-Smith (posthumous), the citation simply stating, '*These officers volunteered for work in uniform behind the enemy lines and were introduced into France by clandestine means. By their gallantry, military skill and devotion to duty they made a notable contribution towards the liberation of France.*' Five years later, on 21 April 1950, it was announced in the *London Gazette* that Colin Ogden-Smith was also awarded the Territorial Efficiency Decoration.

After his time with the Jeds, Guy Le Borgne served with French SAS units in Belgium and Holland. He remained in the French Army after the war and joined a parachute regiment. He and his wife Germaine remained in touch with the Ogden-Smiths for several years after the war and Wendy was only too pleased to exchange letters and gifts with Germaine. Le Borgne would go on to become a general, serving in the First Indochina War and the Algerian War before he retired in 1980 after forty years of service. He ended his career as a military governor of Lyon with the rank

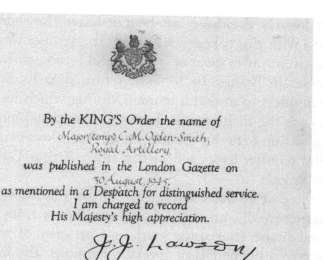

By the KING'S Order the name of
Major (temp) C.M. Ogden-Smith,
Royal Artillery,
was published in the London Gazette on
30 August 1945,
as mentioned in a Despatch for distinguished service.
I am charged to record
His Majesty's high appreciation.

J.J. Lawson

Secretary of State for War

15. The certificate confirming the Mention in Despatches awarded posthumously to Ogden-Smith after the war.

of *général de corps d'armée*, having been appointed a Grand Officier de la Légion d'Honneur to add to his Croix de Guerre awarded by the French and a Military Cross awarded by the British for his gallantry in north-west Europe. Guy Le Borgne died in 2007, aged eighty-seven.

After his mission with Francis, Arthur Dallow remained with the Jeds and went out to the Far East where he served in Burma with Force 136. He was awarded the Military Medal in 1945 for his gallantry, at the age of just twenty-one. After the war he left the army and initially struggled to settle down. Along with some friends he raised enough money to buy a boat but their attempt to sail from Scotland to the South Pacific resulted in them being rescued by the coastguard; a second attempt later ended in the same result! He later worked in an engineering company and settled in Bristol, where he ended up running a factory. When the factory closed down he decided not to be transferred elsewhere and set up a business with two colleagues instead. The venture worked well and Dallow went on to become a successful businessman with several businesses in Bristol. In 1987 he returned to Kerbozec with his two daughters to attend a reunion, during which he met up once again with the Fiche family. It was an emotional reunion and the deep affection between the former comrades was evident for all to see. The reunion happened just in time: Arthur Dallow died the following year.

At the end of the war Ogden-Smith's widow, Wendy, and his parents received a number of poignant letters from France. Tony returned home after three years as a prisoner of war and Bruce had survived his period of special operations. The family could at least take comfort from the warmth and gratitude of the people of Querrien and for what Ogden-Smith had done towards the liberation of France. Amongst the many letters to Wendy was one written by the young Louis Fiche, which included photos taken by Guyader at Kerbozec at the end of the war, showing the scene where her husband had died. On the back of each photograph was a brief explanation of the picture written in French: the first had been taken from near the ruins of the farmhouse and showed the general area where the men had been in hiding; the second showed the shallow ditch where they had been when the Germans arrived; the third showed the point where Ogden-Smith had tried to escape over the hedge and then fell mortally wounded at the base of a tree; and the fourth showed his temporary burial site after the Germans had left. For the first time Wendy could see for herself where her husband had spent the last moments of his life.

The farm at Kerbozec had remained in a state of almost ruin until the end of the war and for several months the Fiche family were left to live in quite difficult conditions. Eliane recalls: 'It was some refugees from Lorient and living at Belle Fontaine who produced iron bedsteads for the three of us; my mother, myself and my cousin, André Burbaud, who was still with us because at that time Paris had still not been liberated. André left in September with his father who had cycled all the way from Paris to fetch him. When the Germans had gone, Guy Le Borgne requisitioned a German 'barraque', which was a prefabricated dwelling with three rooms and painted green. Once again, it was the refugees who put it up. We received furniture which the Germans had left behind, also a cooking stove. Beforehand we had to prepare our meals in a barn without a roof.'

The bodies of Colin Ogden-Smith, Louis Fiche and Maurice Miodon were exhumed from their temporary burial site at the farm on 13 August 1944 and given a proper burial two days later at the cemetery in Querrien: Ogden-Smith in a plot next to Louis Fiche. Then, in 1946, and in a quite remarkable and unparalleled gesture of gratitude, the French community decided they wanted to bury Colin Ogden-Smith in the cemetery at Guiscriff with other members of the *Maquis*, in a private vault alongside the bodies of Maurice Miodon and Gérard Gaultier de Carville. The first the Ogden-Smith family knew of the idea was when they received a letter from the father of de Carville. In his letter dated 15 April 1946, Monsieur R Gaultier de Carville wrote:

Sir, Allow me to introduce myself. I am the father of Lieutenant Gérard Gaultier de Carville, head of the underground of Guiscriff and combat friend of your son Major Ogden-Smith. With the mother of Maurice Miodon, who died with Major Ogden-Smith, we have decided to build a vault at Guiscriff so we could put together the bodies of our two sons, and if you wish the one of Major Ogden-Smith. It is not only our wish but also the one of the Guiscriff underground. It is also the wish of Captain Le Borgne whom you know well. In matter of fact the whole population of Guiscriff considers these three heroes as their property and wish to keep them close. Coming back from deportation I went for a pilgrimage to my son's grave and I had the intention of bringing my son's body back to the family vault but faced with this touching desire I decided to leave him in his underground world. On her side, the mother of Maurice Miodon has taken the same decision, judging that in Guiscriff they will

be with the people who loved them and who will honour them. If your
thinking agrees with ours you should send us official authorisation and it
is understood we will on our side inform you of all proceedings.

Although it could not have been an easy decision, the Ogden-Smith family agreed to the request and the reinterment of Colin Ogden-Smith took place at Guiscriff Communal Cemetery on 28 July 1946, the second anniversary of his death. For whatever reason, no member of the Ogden-Smith family attended the service – they were, however, represented by a British lady, Mrs M K Fullerton, who was a friend of Maurice Miodon and lived in France. The service was attended by a huge number of people, reported to be in the thousands, each of them looking as if it was their own personal tragedy. In the church the priest broke off in French in his sermon and continued in English: 'We highly appreciate the honour conferred upon us today. We are officially entrusted with the guard over the relics of three heroes. Your dead are under good guard. Death itself has not parted them from each other. Their example shall not be forgotten and the monument erected in their honour in our cemetery will tell our children for years and years to come: show to old friendships and like those who are lying in this tomb, be always ready to fight for right and freedom.'

The British national anthem was also played and, after the service, the three representatives of each family walked behind the cars to the cemetery just a short distance away – the road down which they walked, the Rue de Scaer, was packed several deep with members of the local community. Flowers were then placed on the grave and on top of the flowers was a card written by Ogden-Smith's father to the Mayor of Querrien, which simply said – '*Commemorating 29 July 1944 at Kerbozec when our son, Major Colin Ogden-Smith, fell with his French comrades in defence of liberty. Vive la France.*'

The three men were now buried and commemorated side by side: Colin Ogden-Smith in the centre with Gérard Gaultier de Carville to his left and Maurice Miodon to his right. There then followed more poignant letters of gratitude to the family. One was from Mrs Fullerton who had represented the Ogden-Smith family at the service. That same day she wrote to Ogden-Smith's widow, Wendy:

Today the reinterment of your husband took place and I attended partly as Maurice's friend but representing your family, being the only British person present. And I was very proud to do so. I must try to see you when I come to England in October to give you an account of what took place today. I cannot hope to pass on anything like the intensity of the emotional effects of the whole thing – it was quite imposing – it was simplicity itself – it was touching beyond anything and there was charm and devotion. There must have been several thousand people there – and they all looked as if it were their own personal tragedy. The flowers were heaped on the grave – yes it is the same stone brought from Querrien to Guiscriff - and I took some of the cards from the wreaths that were for Colin – thinking it might please you. I think now it was the right thing to move them and have them all together here at Guiscriff. You would think so too I know. How perfectly lovely everyone has been. Such kindness tact and charm I have never seen before. Hundreds of people from here send their sympathy.

Shortly after the service, Louis Fiche wrote to Ogden-Smith's father:

I thank you for the wire you sent me in commemoration of the death of your son and of my father. Two years ago, in a common action we were together fighting against the foe we hated with the same mind. Today we are together and we shall stay forever in the same pain. It is in such cases, in spite of their sadness, that we got our mutual friendship, for now and forever I hope. That is our only consolation but it is a deep one. It is because we have the same ideal, and were doing the same job, although with different ways. I leave you now, and thank you more from my mother, sister and myself, for the thought you had for us in so sad an anniversary.

In 1948 the Graves Registration and Imperial War Graves Commission, entrusted with the duty of permanently commemorating those members of the armed forces who had died in the Allied cause, wrote to Wendy Ogden-Smith, asking if the body of her husband should be repatriated. But there was no desire to repatriate Colin. He was at rest in a place where his grave would be tended to and cared for by the local population for generations to come; Colin Ogden-Smith would never be forgotten, at least not by the people of Guiscriff and Querrien.

Wendy then settled in West Sussex and for a while she kept in touch with Le Borgne's wife, Germaine, but their lives gradually moved on. Wendy died in 2001. Charmian spent her last years living a quiet life on the edge of the beautiful South Downs of West Sussex. She never forgot her father but had never been to the site where he died or where he lies buried today. After hearing about the service commemorating the 68th anniversary of her father's death, she was contemplating a visit to Querrien and Guiscriff for the 70th anniversary in 2014. Whether she would have got there or not will sadly never be known; Charmian died suddenly in 2012.

In the immediate aftermath of Ogden-Smith's death there had been some confusion back at SOE headquarters in London about the date and circumstances of his death;[35] even Colin Gubbins, the head of the SOE, had asked to be informed in detail of the circumstances in which Ogden-Smith had died. On the SOE battle casualty form raised, the date of death was initially given as an approximation of 1 August 1944, although the confusion can simply be put down to the lack of information coming from France. The last confirmation that Ogden-Smith had been alive had been received on 27 July, when he was reported as being in the Quimperlé area. Francis had then gone into hiding the following day and then on 29 July the battle at Kerbozec had taken place. The next London knew was on 2 August when a cipher was sent from Giles, reporting the death of Ogden-Smith, and three days later a cipher was received from Dallow, who now had a fully functional radio set again, confirming what Giles had reported earlier.

After the battle of Kerbozec it had not taken long for the *Maquis* to find out what had led to the events at the farm that fateful day in July 1944. A Belgian living nearby had been a collaborator, and while out walking that day he had spotted the members of Francis in their hide at the farm. He had then sent a woman, reported to be his wife, to Quimperlé to alert the *Feldgendarmes* and it was she that Ogden-Smith had seen arriving at the farmhouse in the German staff car. Within days of the battle, the *Maquis* had condemned the Belgian collaborator, his wife and their son to death. Although the teenage son was subsequently spared, the Belgian and his wife were executed by the *Maquis* six days after the battle had taken place. Years later, in 1955, the *Bourgemestre* of Erpe in Belgium wrote to the Mayor of Querrien enquiring about the death of a thirty-year-old Belgian man, Jean-Baptiste-Evariste Moereels, and asked if there were any details relating to the cause of the Belgian's death or if he had been admitted to hospital and subsequently died. In his reply, the Mayor of Querrien simply explained that the man and a woman, named as Anna Le Theoff, were both executed on the evening of 4 August 1944 for informing on the *Maquis* to the Germans.

As for the Germans present at the battle of Kerbozec that day, two of those serving with 609 Feldgendarmerie de Quimperlé became the subject of an investigation after the war. Both had witnessed the killing of Ogden-Smith and Miodon, and one had then ordered the brutal murder of the elderly farmer Fiche and the looting and burning of the farmhouse. In his final report on Francis, submitted in September 1944, Guy Le Borgne had cited two names of German soldiers known to the French for committing atrocities in the area. One of those names was well known to the French and kept recurring after liberation in witness statements describing similar atrocities. Once the war was over, allegations against members of the Feldgendarmerie de Quimperlé continued and included the events at Kerbozec on 29 July 1944.

Of particular interest to the British was the allegation that Major Colin Ogden-Smith had been murdered after being captured alive or, at least, that his body had been maltreated after death. At the end of 1945 it was decided that an investigation into his death, and the other alleged atrocities committed on the farm that day, would be carried out by the Judge Advocate General's War Crimes Investigation Unit based in Germany as part of the British Army of the Rhine. After much correspondence and discussion, it was decided that the alleged crimes were: the mutilation of the dead body of a British national (Ogden-Smith); the murder of a wounded French national – army (Miodon); the murder of a French national – civilian (Fiche); and the burning and looting of a French farm (Kerbozec). The two men specifically named as the accused were Oberfeldwebel Walter Rubsam, who had commanded the *Feldgendarmes* on the day, and his assistant, Oberfeldwebel Eugen Schneider.

In early 1946 the investigation was carried out by two officers of the WCIU: one British, Captain W R Durndell of the East Surrey Regiment, and one Belgian, Captain M A J De Ferrare. During the investigation twenty-seven people, a mix of French and German, were interviewed. One of those interviewed was Doctor Emile-Jean Auffret who had examined the three bodies in the immediate aftermath of the battle at Kerbozec. In his statement regarding Ogden-Smith, sworn before the WCIU and dated 30 January 1946, Doctor Auffret stated:[36]

> *The medical examination revealed a large wound in the umbilical region from which the bowels were emerging. These were not perforated; it is rather likely that the injuries were caused by an edged tool rather than by bullets or grenade splinters. I do not think he had sustained any other injuries.*

Regarding his examination of Maurice Miodon and Louis Fiche, Doctor Auffret stated:[37]

The French soldier had his left leg bandaged and several bullet marks in the head. Fiche had a bullet wound in the chest under the key bone, a wound which was not fatal. At the level of the last six ribs on the right, on the line of the axillary line, a wide and deep wound which had perforated the pleura and the lung, a wound which was certainly caused by a bayonet and which caused the death.

As part of their investigation the two officers visited Kerbozec in early February to talk with Marie-Jeanne Fiche. Eliane remembers: 'We had a visit at Kerbozec of the Intelligence Service, two young handsome people who spoke good French. They asked many questions of my mother and then they went to the cemetery at Querrien. They opened the two coffins and when they returned they told us what they had seen. They asked for some boiling water and some milk, they had a teapot with them. They made some tea and shared it with us. It was a ray of sunshine despite their sad task.'

In addition to their visit to Kerbozec the two officers had been to the Moulin de Kerlévéné to speak to François Naour and at the cemetery at Querrien, Doctor André Jude had carried out an autopsy on Ogden-Smith and Miodon in the presence of a number of witnesses. In his report the doctor concluded that the large hole in Ogden-Smith's stomach had probably been caused by a jagged edge, typically associated with a weapon such as a bayonet, and that his body had probably been maltreated after death.[38]

Walter Rubsam and Eugen Schneider were arrested in April as war criminals in connection with the killing of Ogden-Smith; Rubsam was detained at Le Cordray Pas Chartres and Schneider was arrested at his home in Mannheim, Germany.[39] They were both then interviewed at the beginning of May. Rubsam stated that he was only at the farm as the head of the *Feldgendarmes*, although he did eventually admit to giving the order to burn the farm, and Schneider, as Rubsam's second-in-command, denied any responsibility at all.

The following month the WCIU concluded its investigation and completed its report. The report stated that many of those interviewed claimed that Ogden-Smith had been killed as a result of the severe wounds to his stomach but no one had actually witnessed his death. Just five yards from his body were two prominent trees; one was covered with bullet holes and scarred by shrapnel and at the foot of the tree were blood stains. Apart from the gaping hole in his stomach there were no other visible signs of wounds or injuries. As for Miodon, the report stated that circumstantial evidence tended to show that he was killed after being wounded and captured, and stated that he had been shot in the head. Regarding Fiche, five of the German soldiers that had taken part in the action at Kerbozec had been interviewed but the investigation was unable to obtain any evidence as to how he was killed. All the report could do was to confirm that Fiche had been shot at close range, although this wound would not have been fatal and that it had been the bayonet wound that had killed him. The report also stated that it had been impossible to determine which soldiers had actually committed the atrocities and, therefore, the case was based on the responsibility of command. The investigating officers were of the opinion that both of the accused were unwilling to tell the truth and it had only been after considerable questioning that Rubsam had finally admitted to giving the order to burn the farm. In view of this, and of the general character of the men given by the French witnesses, it was obvious to the investigating officers that the two accused knew far more than they would reveal. The report concluded:

> *It would seem from the evidence that Major Ogden-Smith was killed fairly in battle; but there is every possibility that his body was maltreated after death.*

Amongst the report's recommendations was the suggestion that contact should be made with the French War Crimes at Rennes because Rubsam and Schneider were well known in the area and were wanted by the French.[40]

The report was then sent from the Judge Advocate General's office to London[41] with a short note informing the SOE that:

This case has now been fully investigated by WCIU in Germany and it is quite clear that Major Ogden-Smith was killed in action. Further, that the SAS man, who was in fact killed after action, was in fact a French subject. In these circumstances, while there is a clear case against the two German accused, the papers are being handed over to the French authorities for trial.

In July there was brief talk of reinvestigating the case regarding Ogden-Smith's death when it was thought further information suggested that Ogden-Smith might have been killed in different circumstances.[42] An investigator contacted No 1 MREU (Missing Research and Enquiry Unit) but there was no further evidence and nothing more could be said about the case. In December 1946, the commanding officer of the WCIU concluded:[43]

It is thought that no useful purpose would be served in reinvestigating this case as none of the information contained in the MREU report contradicts the evidence submitted in the unit report where the manner in which Major Ogden-Smith met his death was fully described. May I therefore consider this case closed.

As far as the other alleged crimes against the French were concerned, it appears that Walter Rubsam was later tried by the French in Paris in his absence during 1952 and received a sentence of five years' imprisonment, although this is unconfirmed.

Post-war accounts of team Francis and the events at Kerbozec have come up with variations of Colin Ogden-Smith's death. One account suggests he was captured alive and then finished off with a bullet to the head while another suggestion is that he chose to end his own life by taking cyanide rather than to be captured alive. While the reasons for both accounts are understandable, neither the affidavit of Doctor Emile-Jean Auffret nor the autopsy report by Doctor André Jude support either of these suggestions.

The first account, stating that Ogden-Smith was captured alive and finished off with a bullet to the head, will have come from the file on team Francis held at The National Archives, where, in his report on returning to England, Arthur Dallow states this to be the case. Dallow also states that Miodon was killed by the Germans but makes no mention of the Frenchman being shot in the head. Rather interestingly, Guy Le Borgne's report states it was the other way round and that Ogden-Smith 'was deliberately shot by the Germans' but makes no reference to him being shot in the head, while his account of Miodon's death clearly states the Frenchman was 'finished off with a bullet in the temple'.

There is clearly a contradiction and reflects what each man believed at the time but this is almost certainly because of what they had been told in the aftermath of Kerbozec rather than being based on anything else. In any event, the suggestion that Ogden-Smith was finished off with a bullet in the head can quickly be discounted as it was, in fact, Miodon whose life ended this way. Doctor Auffret and Doctor Jude were both clear in describing the cause of death of Miodon, who was captured alive and mercilessly finished off with bullets to the head, and neither doctor would have had any reason not to report similarly had Ogden-Smith suffered the same fate. Furthermore, when Doctor Auffret examined the body of Ogden-Smith in the aftermath of the battle, an event witnessed by Marie-Jeanne and Eliane Fiche, there were no visible signs of a bullet to the head and in his affidavit Auffret states that apart from the obvious 'large wound in the umbilical region' he had 'not seen any other wounds'.

The second suggestion that Ogden-Smith chose to end his own life by taking cyanide rather than to be captured alive would have come from comments made after the war that small fragments of what appeared like glass were seen next to his body. Whether Ogden-Smith opted to take an L-pill with him when he parachuted into France is not known; some did, but others did not – it was a matter of personal choice. Again, when Doctor Auffret examined his body in the aftermath of the battle there were no visible signs of cyanide having been taken nor was there any mention of the possible use of cyanide in his affidavit. The fragments seen near his body could have been from anything but it is almost certain they were from the morphine syrettes used by Ogden-Smith prior to his death; the report by the WCIU supports this explanation as it confirms that empty morphine syrettes were found near his body.

While on the subject of morphine, it is worth noting that the contents of both syrettes in Ogden-Smith's first-aid kit would have been a massive dose for anyone to endure. The British issued Omnopon (similar to morphine tartrate used by the Americans, with the difference being the addition of codeine and papaveretum) and the standard dose was half a grain (30 mg), which itself would be a large dose considering that, in current palliative care, a patient never having had the drug before would be started on 5–10 mg every four hours. Twice the standard dose would have been massive.

It is impossible to know for certain what happened in the last moments of Ogden-Smith's life. No one from team Francis witnessed his death and none of the Germans interviewed by the WCIU offered any further information. But when taking everything into account, it is almost certain that it was the combination of his terrible wounds, which could well have proved fatal anyway, and the huge dose of morphine that ended his life. He certainly died before Miodon, and the Frenchman clearly prevented the Germans from closing in on the two of them for some time. Ogden-Smith was almost certainly dead before the Germans reached him and if anything did happen after that, which led to the investigation by the WCIU, it happened without Colin being aware.

As for Kerbozec, reconstruction of the farmhouse began in 1946. Marie-Jeanne Fiche and her husband Louis had long planned to build a modern house on the farm, but sadly only Marie-Jeanne would see their dreams become reality. The plans were still with the architect and so work began. Beautiful chestnut trees were felled to provide the wood and the new farmhouse was eventually finished in 1948.

It was never going to be possible for Marie-Jeanne and Eliane to run the farm; besides, Eliane did not wish to stay at the farm, and her brother Louis had moved out. For a number of years Kerbozec was managed by Marie-Jeanne's eldest son René, who had not been present at the farm in July 1944. The farm was later let to another family before Marie-Jeanne finally decided to sell in 1974, when she was eighty-four years old. Many changes were subsequently made to the farm: trees were planted on the prairies; the small brook, which had been named after Guyader, was filled in; and the slope of the land was levelled – although the site where the battle had taken place and the tree beneath which Ogden-Smith had died were left untouched. The new owners of Kerbozec were always very kind to Marie-Jeanne and agreed to let her stay at the farm, with her own bedroom and kitchen, for the rest of her life. In 1985, at the age of ninety-six, Marie-Jeanne was awarded the Legion d'Honneur for her extreme courage during the Second World War when she sheltered members of the *Maquis* and team Francis at her farm. Poignantly, the award was presented to her by Général Guy Le Borgne. Eventually age got the better of Marie-Jeanne: it was no longer possible for her to live at the farm and, having just celebrated her one hundredth birthday, she finally moved into a home. The fearless Marie-Jeanne Fiche died at the age of 105.

The younger Louis Fiche remained in the area after the war and later ran a model shop in Quimper. He died in 2004. Eliane also remained in the local area and still lives in Querrien. After Ogden-Smith's body was moved to Guiscriff in 1946, she bought the vacated plot next to her father and later had her own husband, Guy Lebas, buried in the plot when he died in 2002. Although she is now in her eighties, Eliane's memories of the German occupation and the horrors of 29 July 1944 are still very much fresh in her mind. The loss of her father and that of Colin Ogden-Smith is no less painful now than it was seventy years ago.

Two of the three crosses made by Marie-Jeanne in 1944 still survive and can be found together on communal land just a few yards from the entrance to Kerbozec. Eliane explains:

In 1944 my mother had three crosses made and placed them where our three Martyrs had fallen. Later she moved the Miodon cross, placed it alongside the road opposite where the German lorries arrived on 29 July. She found an engraver to make a plaque with the names of the three victims. Kerbozec was sold in 1974. In order to build a barn the new owners moved the cross, the community tidied it up and put it on a plinth. Time passed, all the good land had been sold, and the house was sold, leaving the new owner with a square of lawn and some non-fertile land. My father's monument was in a field, it no doubt 'got in the way' and disappeared. I think it was almost certainly placed on marshy ground some metres from the place where he was slain. The Major's cross did not bother anyone. It was at the foot of the tree where he had so gallantly fallen. In 2008 the Mayor, his adjoint and I considered it merited a better fate. It was placed nicely on some private land and there was a ceremony. In spite of the land owner's good intentions he was not too happy with the situation as it meant people entering his property, not a good idea! We have found it easier to start again and put the two monuments together. The land is communal which is important.

Today, seventy years on, the farmhouse at Kerbozec remains privately owned and the garden is beautifully maintained. The field leading down to where Francis had been in hiding, and where Ogden-Smith was killed, belongs to a nearby farm. It is as tranquil now as it would have been before the Second World War and life has long returned to the peaceful way it would have been before the German occupation. The only sounds that can be heard in the fields of the farm tend to come from the machinery that has long replaced the horse and cart. Seventy years of woodland growth has changed the appearance of the location but the main features are still all there: the farmhouse, the sloped field, the farm tracks and even the tree where Ogden-Smith spent the last moments of his life, all provide poignant reminders of what took place.

But it is not the place that has kept this story alive. It is the French community. The letters sent to Ogden-Smith's family after his death all reflect the strength of feeling and gratitude of the local French community at the time. The subsequent desire to keep Ogden-Smith buried in France, and to have him lie alongside his brave young French comrades, Miodon and de Carville, provide further evidence of just how highly the French regarded the courage and sacrifice of the *Major Anglais*.

16.   Having just laid a wreath at the grave of Ogden-Smith at Guiscriff, the author stands while Eliane Lebas reads a short prayer of remembrance. Other members of the local community have gathered for what turned out to be an impromptu moment of poignancy.

In 1947, the year after the bodies of Ogden-Smith and Miodon were reinterred at Guiscriff Communal Cemetery, the local French community held a short service at Kerbozec to remember the three men who had fallen at the farm on 29 July 1944. The service held that day marked the third anniversary of what the locals have since called the Battle of Kerbozec. Quite remarkably and most poignantly, the service is still held today.

On 28 July 2012, I was delighted to accompany two members of the Ogden-Smith family, Angela Weston and Sam Gardner, the daughter and grand-daughter of Colin's brother, Bruce Ogden-Smith, and four members of the Royal Air Force, to Kerbozec to attend the service marking the 68th anniversary of the battle. It was a quite remarkable scene, with the narrow country lane filled by more than a hundred members of the local community, their ranks adorned by the flags and colours of France.

Attending the ceremony was a mix of veterans, members of the local community, invited dignitaries and other guests. Among those standing there were Eliane Lebas, the daughter of the elderly farmer Louis Fiche, who had been on the farm that fateful day and who had heard the battle and witnessed its aftermath, Louis Kervédou, the farmhand at Lopers where Ogden-Smith had first established contact with the French, and Denise Le Moine, whose father, Francis Le Quéré, had allowed Francis to shelter at his farm at Fornigou. Eliane, Louis and Denise had all been teenagers during July 1944 and they had all met Colin Ogden-Smith during his brief time in France, and all three had been warmed by his kindness and compassion. I was also fortunate to meet many others, including Armelle Burbaud, whose father André had been staying at the farm on that fateful day, and Yves Naour, the son of François Naour, the miller at Moulin de Kerlévéné.

After the short ceremony was over the locals and invited guests gathered together outside the farmhouse to enjoy a glass or two in a typical display of French hospitality, sharing their own thoughts and memories of the past. I felt privileged to spend a few private moments with Eliane. We strolled a few yards away from the gathering and stood together looking down across the field to the point where Francis had been in hiding. It was a beautiful day and there was silence; neither of us said a word. Eliane then looked up towards the sky and then looked at me. She smiled. She did not say a word, but then she did not need to. The events of 29 July 1944 have lived in her memory ever since. They always will.

Notes

1 J E Appleyard, *Geoffrey, The Story of Apple*, Blandford Press Ltd, London, 1947, p. 55,

2 *Ibid.*, p. 56.

3 Hilary St George Saunders, *The Green Beret: The Story of the Commandos, 1940-45*, New English Library, 1968, but first published by Michael Joseph Ltd, Great Britain 1949, p. 63.

4 The tanks were Matildas of the 7th Royal Tank Regiment.

5 St George Saunders, *The Green Beret.*

6 *Ibid.*, p. 64. The sergeant quoted is reported as Sergeant Charles Stewart, although it is not known which unit he was from.

7 TNA, WO 218/168, War Diary Layforce 'A' Battalion (No 7 Commando), Jan–May 1941.

8 TNA, WO 218/158, Middle East Commando Depot, Jan–Dec 1941.

9 Extract from personal letter from Captain Jocelyn Nicholls to his mother in 1942, held in the author's private collection.

10 Appleyard, *Geoffrey*, p. 155.

11 TNA, DEFE 2/109 – SSRF file including Operation Branford.

12 *Ibid.*

13 Account taken from Winston G Ramsey, *The War in the Channel Islands, Then and Now*, p. 149.

14 *Ibid.*, p. 154.

15 *Ibid.*

16 *Ibid.*

17 *Ibid.*

18 Appleyard, *Geoffrey*, p. 128.

19 Chief of the Imperial General Staff, General Sir Alan Brooke.

20 Report by Capt C M Ogden-Smith RA, dated 11 October 1943, now filed in TNA, HS 9/1377/2 SOE Personnel File – Colin Malcolm Ogden-Smith.

21 SOE's operating authority for North Africa.

22 Confidential Report on Capt C M Ogden-Smith RA (D/H181) by Commanding Officer 11 SOD, dated 5 October 1943, now filed in TNA, HS 9/1377/2 SOE Personnel File – Colin Malcolm Ogden-Smith.

23 Report by Capt C M Ogden-Smith RA, dated 11 October 1943, now filed in TNA, HS 9/1377/2 SOE Personnel File – Colin Malcolm Ogden-Smith.

24 The name Jedburgh simply came from an approved list of code words rather than having any link to the Scottish Borders town of the same name.

25 TNA, HS 6/507 SOE France – Jedburghs – Team Francis 1.

26 *Ibid.*

27 *Ibid.*

28 TNA, HS 6/507 SOE France – Jedburghs – Team Francis 1. Report by Sgt Dallow.

29 Filed in TNA, HS 6/507 SOE France – Jedburghs – Team Francis 1.

30 TNA, HS 6/507 SOE France – Jedburghs – Team Francis 1. Report by Capitaine Le Zachmeur on the death of Major Ogden-Smith and Maurice Miodon SAS.

31 Although Le Borgne reported the farmer to be seventy-two years old, he was in fact seventy-one.

32 Although Le Borgne reports the execution of the Belgian, his wife and his son; the son, still in his teens, was subsequently spared. The executions were actually carried out on the evening of 4 August and not two days later as stated in the report.

33 TNA, HS 6/507 SOE France – Jedburghs – Team Francis 1. Report by Sgt Dallow.

34 TNA, HS 9/1377/2 SOE Personnel File – Colin Malcolm Ogden-Smith – FFI Citation des Jedburghs, 91977 Ogden-Smith, Colin Malcolm by Lt Col D L G Carlton-Smith for a posthumous Legion d'Honneur.

35 TNA, HS 9/1377/2 SOE Personnel File – Colin Malcolm Ogden-Smith, SOE Battle Casualty Form.

36 Production (witness) No 13 of the Report by War Crimes Investigation Unit B.A.O.R. dated 10 May 1946 now filed in WO 309/843 JAG BAOR War Crimes Group – Querrien, France – Killing of a British Officer, 1946.

37 *Ibid.*

38 Production (witness) No 21 of the Report by War Crimes Investigation Unit B.A.O.R. dated 10 May 1946 now filed in WO 309/843 JAG BAOR War Crimes Group – Querrien, France – Killing of a British Officer, 1946.

39 Military Government of Germany, War Criminal Arrest Report, Eugen Schneider, now filed in WO 309/843 JAG BAOR War Crimes Group – Querrien, France – Killing of a British Officer, 1946.

40 Conclusions and Recommendation in the Report by War Crimes Investigation Unit B.A.O.R. dated 10 May 1946 now filed in WO 309/843 JAG BAOR War Crimes Group – Querrien, France – Killing of a British Officer, 1946.

41 Loose Minute from AG 3 (VW) D.A.A.G. to MO 1 (SP) titled 'Alleged Murder of Major Ogden-Smith' dated 27 May 1946 now filed in WO 309/843 JAG BAOR War Crimes Group – Querrien, France – Killing of a British Officer, 1946.

42 Loose Minute from AG 3B (VW) D.A.A.G. to MO 1 (SP) titled 'Alleged Murder of Major Ogden-Smith' dated 8 July 1946 now filed in WO 309/843 JAG BAOR War Crimes Group – Querrien, France – Killing of a British Officer, 1946.

43 BAOR/WC/C/14 to DJAG (WCS) Subject 'Alleged War Crimes at Finistere' dated 16 December 1946 now filed in WO 309/843 JAG BAOR War Crimes Group – Querrien, France – Killing of a British Officer, 1946.

Bibliography, Sources And References

Published Sources

Appleyard, J E, *Geoffrey* (Blandford Press, London, 1947)

Ashcroft, Michael, *Special Forces Heroes* (Headline Review, London, 2008)

Beavan, Colin, *Operation Jedburgh* (Penguin, New York, 2006)

Binney, Marcus, *Secret War Heroes* (Hodder & Stoughton, London, 2006)

Boyce, Fredric and Everett, Douglas, *SOE: The Scientific Secrets* (History Press, Stroud, 2009)

Cado, Marcel, *Querrien* (Liv' Éditions et la Marie de Querrien, France, 1998)

de la Billière, General Sir Peter, *Supreme Courage* (Little, Brown, London, 2004)

Dunning, James, *When Shall Their Glory Fade?* (Frontline, London, 2011)

Ford, Roger, *Fire From The Forest* (Cassell, London, 2003)

Ford, Roger, *Steel From The Sky* (Orion Publishing, London, 2004)

Irwin, Lt Col (Ret'd) Will, *The Jedburghs* (Public Affairs, Cambridge, MA, 2005)

Lett, Brian, *The Small Scale Raiding Force* (Pen & Sword Military, Barnsley, 2013)

McCue, Paul, *SAS Operation Bulbasket* (Pen & Sword Military, Barnsley, 2009)

Owen, James, *Commando* (Little, Brown, London, 2012)

Ramsey, Winston G, *The War in the Channel Islands, Then and Now* (Battle of Britain Prints International Limited, London, 1981)

Scott, Michael, *Special Forces Commander* (Pen & Sword Military, Barnsley, 2011)

St George Saunders, Hilary, *The Green Beret: The Story of the Commandos 1940–45* (New English Library, 1968 but first published by Michael Joseph Ltd, Great Britain, 1949)

The National Archives

ADM 179/227, SSRF – Operation Aquatint

DEFE 2/109, SSRF – Operations Barricade, Dryad, Branford, Aquatint, Basalt, Batman

HS 6/507, SOE France – Jedburghs – Team Francis 1

HS 7/236-7, SOE Massingham North Africa War Diaries 1943

HS 9/1377/2, SOE Personnel File – Colin Malcolm Ogden-Smith

WO 106/4417, Early Planning of the SSRF

WO 218/152, War Diaries – No 3 Special Service Battalion, 1 November 1940 – 28 February 1941

WO 218/158, War Diaries – Middle East Commando Depot, 1 January – 31 December 1941

WO 218/168, War Diaries – Layforce, A Battalion, 1 January – 31 May 1941

WO 309/843, JAG BAOR War Crimes Group - Querrien, France – Killing of a British Officer, 1946

Unpublished Sources

Irwin, Major Wyman W, 'A Special Force: Origin and Development of the Jedburgh Project in Support of Operation Overlord', thesis presented to the US Army Command and General Staff College, released 1991.

Journal de Marche – Forces Françaises de l'Intérieur, Arrondissement de Quimperlé.

Other Sources

Much of what has been written in this book has come from the personal accounts of those who were there or from family members or others who have all helped contribute to this book. These sources of information are listed below:

Personal diary of Colin Ogden-Smith.

Personal letters of the Ogden-Smith family.

Personal letters of Captain Jocelyn Nicholls.

Personal memoirs of Guy Le Borgne.

Personal memoirs of Eliane Lebas.

Family memories of Arthur Dallow (via Ann Dallow (now Ann Taig), Elizabeth Dallow and Matt Dallow).

Family memories of André Burbaud (via Armelle Burbaud).

Various articles and correspondence from Marcel Moysan, the Mayor of Querrien.

Various articles and correspondence from Marc le Meur.

Various articles and correspondence from Gérard Flatrès.

Index

Because of numerous changes throughout the war, ranks have been omitted and only the names of those individuals included in this book are included in the index.